My
American
Adventure
(2024)

My American Adventure
Copyright © 2024 by Rita Abiamiri MSN, RN, CCRN

Published in the United States of America

Library of Congress Control Number: 2023923385
ISBN   Paperback: 979-8-89091-539-9
ISBN   eBook: 979-8-89091-540-5

All rights reserved. No part of this publication may be reproduced, stored in a retrieval system or transmitted in any way by any means, electronic, mechanical, photocopy, recording or otherwise without the prior permission of the author except as provided by USA copyright law.

The opinions expressed by the author are not necessarily those of ReadersMagnet, LLC.

ReadersMagnet, LLC
10620 Treena Street, Suite 230 | San Diego, California, 92131 USA
1.619. 354. 2643 | www.readersmagnet.com

Book design copyright © 2024 by ReadersMagnet, LLC. All rights reserved.

Cover design by Jhiee Oraiz
Interior design by Don De Guzman

My American Adventure (2024)

A taste of discrimination and prejudice in America through the eyes of an American Immigrant

RITA ABIAMIRI
MSN, RN, CCRN

Foreword

I am delighted to write this foreword, not only because the author, Rita Abiamiri is my big sister and most reliable mentor from childhood, but also because I believe deeply in the value of sharing her American adventure and experience it would bring to the reader; whether as advanced notice to aspiring African immigrants, as a benchmarking resource for existing immigrants, or as educational and entertainment resource for people born in American who have the desire to learn about cultural diversity and experiences of foreigners who ventured to leave their home countries to come and settle in the United States. What she describes in this book are experiences that generally fly under the radar for most average Americans but are life changing for African immigrants.

I had a glimpse of Rita's early life experience as an immigrant when I spent my summer vacation with her and her family in 1984, about 4 years after she came to USA. She, already at this time, has had a taste of several of the life experiences described in this book. As you page through, you will notice an honest and passionate account of these experiences ranging from how mystified she was when she realized how far from the truth is the way USA is represented on many movies and TV programs she had watched in Nigeria before coming, to how tough it was to make ends meet in USA contrary to popular belief, to the realities of racism and social injustices, just to mention a few. I particularly applaud her courage and tenacity in dealing with many of what life threw at her, from joggling through work while parenting their young children with no help in the early days of her life in USA, to achieving impressive career success while raising three boys fully engrossed in American football, to achieving impressive financial success.

These are no small achievements, because many who have faced similar challenges would either end up as stay-at-home moms (no disparaging implied) or would have had limited success raising their children. Instead, her perseverance, hard work and strong drive toward success and her deep faith, grounded in strong family upbringing, helped her to achieve a long and fruitful professional career in good balance with significant accomplishments in family and financial life. In several chapters, Rita takes us inside her parenting methods, how she handled instances of racial prejudice, workplace harassment and discrimination, and we will also learn about the joy and excitement of reaping the rewards of her hard work when they occurred.

One question that kept recurring throughout the book is her dilemma whether to stay or not to stay, and when is the right time to move back to Nigeria to pursue other opportunities? While it is expected that readers will have varying opinions about this based on their personal perspectives, you will come to learn the complexities of answering that question as Rita takes you through each phase of her life in USA. Additionally, you will come to learn about Rita's take on controversial matters such as poverty, racial injustice, and white supremacy.

Overall, this book is nothing short of a masterpiece: relatable, thought-provoking, captivating and often funny as only Rita can write it. As you read ahead, prepare to be amazed as she helps you navigate through a migration journey that is this meticulously told story of her life "My American Adventure".

Bernard Chukwulebe, PhD.
Chicago, Illinois USA

Why write this book and why now.

I get questions a lot about why I wrote this book. The idea for this book was conceived in my mind throughout my working years in America.

Whenever I went through anything, I perceived to be either discrimination or prejudice. I said in my mind, "One day, I will put these experiences down in a book for the world and my family to read." Over the years, I wrote a couple of paragraphs and never had time to devote to writing it. It just happened that one day in 2020, during the Covid lock down, I had already retired and staying home with family. I was babysitting my grandchildren that day. I had a phone call from a friend who I conversed with in Igbo language. My grandchildren have not learned Igbo language because their parents were not speaking it either. Soon after I dropped the phone, my grandchildren gathered around me and began to query me. "Grandma, tell us what you were saying about Nigeria?" They mimicked some of the Igbo words I said.

That was like a light bulb hitting my head. I thought that then would be a good time to write the book I had in mind - the book that tells my story. Being the Matriarch of my family in the USA, I thought it wise to write this book to create a legacy for my children and my generations ahead which will familiarize them with what I went through hoping that they will not have to go through it themselves. It will teach them about racism that I endured and also help them understand when they become victims of overt or subtle prejudice. It will also teach them the personal struggles we endured from caring for them with no other help. Now they have their own children, they have me babysitting whenever they need. I am only a phone call away whenever they have to go out on the weekend and never have to worry about childcare. Now they say, "It must have been tough not having help in raising us," and appreciate us their parents more.

I had a lot of time to rack my brain to remember a few things and the chronological order of the events. Initially I was not writing to publish a book. As I said earlier, it was a legacy I was to leave for my family. When I completed the manuscript, I sent it to my brother Dr. Benard Chukwulebe to proofread. Dr. Chukwulebe gave a good review of the book and encouraged me to publish it. As mentioned earlier, it was written during the time of Covid lock down. I was at home doing practically nothing. That afforded me the opportunity of time to write it. So read on and be entertained by what you read or gain knowledge of the real-life struggles of an immigrant in America.

Introduction

My mother of blessed memory always said, "No one knows his or her destiny until one gets married and starts building a family." Social scientists are still studying the emotional differences of married and single people to determine which status is more favorable. Most single persons will admit that single life is the better part of adult life as it offers them more freedom to live life any way they want. Married people on the other hand may claim that being married offers more life fulfilment than single life. Destiny of a person is referred to as a predetermined course of events in a person's life, sometimes also referred to as fortune or fate.

A single person generally has responsibility to him or herself (except when that single person bears the responsibility of his/her family when the family is not able). My mother was born and raised in the Royal family of Chief Unegbu Onwuseraka of Umuchiri, Okwe in Imo State of Nigeria. She never thought in her lifetime that she would raise five children all under ten years old alone. I always thought my mother made that statement because she was widowed at a young age and her destiny was revealed to her after she got married and also following the death of her husband, my father. I am not sure if her statement is a universally held belief; however, I believed her statement may be true because I can confidently say my own destiny unraveled after I got married to my husband.

When a person gets married or gets into a relationship, life is no longer about that person alone. The partner must always be considered when making decisions concerning both. They both go through life "in sickness and in health, for richer or poorer till death do them part", as they vowed to each other the day of their marriage. That includes going through good times and adversity together. For example, when the couple goes through events like child-bearing and all that is involved, loosing children, pregnancy or even loosing either of the partner. Good things and bad in relationships are endless, both of them share the burden. I enjoyed my singe life until Sunday January 4th, 1981, when I tied the knot with my husband, Peter.

The wedding took place at my husband's village church…St Joseph's Catholic Church Umunohu, Amakohia Ihitte in Imo State of Nigeria. Our wedding was prepared in a haste. The reason was that after the traditional marriage, my mother would not allow me to join my husband until we were married in the church. Couple not married in the church but living together was frowned at, at that time. My mother, being the head of the Catholic Women Organization (CWO) in Okigwe Parish wanted to show she was a good role model of what she preached. She speculated my husband and I might not marry in the church immediately if she had allowed me to join my husband and she was not going for that. Peter had only one month to stay in Nigeria before going back to the USA. So, we had only three weeks to plan the wedding, get married, and go to the embassy in Lagos for my visa.

Some of the guests from long distance stayed at our house there in the village. It was a two-day celebration and excitement – from Saturday 'till Monday evening when all the guests departed. It appeared everything went fast so much that my attention was focused on making sure every plan was executed well. The wedding turned out to be nice considering the short planning time. It was like any other celebration and I did not realize what was going on until it was all over.

The next morning, Tuesday January 6th, I woke up and looked around the house and the compound. Only my husband and his family members were around. My people and other guests have all left. The reality of what happened hit me. A strange feeling enveloped me! A voice in my head asked and answered, "What just happened? Rita you just got married!" was the reply. Suddenly I remembered my mother's words, "No one knows his or her destiny until one gets married and starts building a family." I thought to myself, my destiny is about to unfold. First, I cried as a feeling of apprehension about

MY AMERICAN ADVENTURE (2024)

what the future holds for my husband and I overwhelmed me. Then I got on my knees to pray. "God, I know you are the giver of all destiny, please give me a perfect destiny. Let my marriage be blessed abundantly. Let my husband and I live in peace. Bless us with long healthy life, and four healthy children: two boys and two girls. Prosper us and help us be a blessing to our family and our community."

Before the wedding, I had no plans to go to America with my husband. My plan was to stay behind since my husband had only two or three years left to complete his doctoral education. The 1980's were the years when going to America was not so glamorous as it came to be years later. Even when the country was still reeling from the aftermath of the Nigerian civil war, Nigeria was still Africa's largest economy and doing well. Since I had a good stable job, I thought it wise to stay back and begin to establish us in Nigeria. But my husband insisted that I came along. He suggested I would like it there. So, we were simultaneously preparing for the wedding and for leaving for the United States soon after the wedding. My visa had already been secured before the wedding and we were all set to go.

On January 16th 1981, we left Nigeria for a journey I considered to be a sojourn. However, years later, this journey that I thought was for a short time would take a lifetime. After over four decades in America, we are now on a crossroad. Returning to Nigeria for good, to my utter dismay has become a disillusionment. Staying in America has also become an illusion. We have spent this many years in America working hard, going through adversities, enduring racial discrimination, and finally achieved relative success. Now we want to return and help our mother land. But deep-rooted corruption has taken over our motherland. "When will we be able to return to Nigeria for good?" has now become a rhetorical question.

For years, we made plans to leave America for good, only to scrap the plan because it was not a good time. "The economy is bad, not a good time" would be the response when we contacted family in Nigeria to inquire about the status of things. For the next ten years, we made numerous efforts to uproot ourselves to return to Nigeria for good. It was never a good time until the children grew up in America denying them growing up in the culture of their root.

It was "not a good time". There were safety issues: kidnappings, corrupt politicians, police corruption and brutality, bad roads, no amenities…electricity, water and so on.

In 2002, we decided to "grab the bull by the horn" and ventured to Nigeria with the children to get the feel of how it would be like. It was very disheartening that we had to hire armed guards to protect us in our own village, the village for that matter! That was the first time we spent time in the house we built years before. The cities turned out to be safer to stay in. "What was the point of going home if the safety issues precluded spending time in the village with our people?" the children asked. The whole idea of going home was to be with their kins, and learn the culture and the language. We spent one month and burned all the money we had, mostly because of the cost associated with the hired guards and other expenses which were not initially anticipated. We went back to America in disappointed spirits. Though the period was too short for the children to have a meaningful exposure to our people, they enjoyed the trip. The children took pride in knowing their root and planned to visit when they are able. After that time, my husband and I periodically visited Nigeria, but never ready to pack up and go for good.

Nor will we be able to pack up the children and go with us. They were all born in America and are American citizens. They are now grown-up adults with families. We are not getting any younger. We now have grey hairs; arthritis is menacing our joints. Aches and pains have become our companions. We have become senior citizens, Social Security and Medicare eligible. These questions have come up in my mind very often as I go about my daily routines. Are we still going back to Nigeria and when? Is my destiny to spend my lifetime in a foreign land where I have now become a citizen? Has my sojourn of the early 80's become a lifetime journey?One cautionary note to the reader: For the people who are planning to go abroad for education, or those who are in diaspora already with hope of returning to Nigeria after your education, bear in mind that you may end up in the sojourner crossroad like we did. Unless you have a job already waiting for you in Nigeria, it may not be easy to leave soon after you completed your education. You may need to spend some time to prepare yourself for the return. The longer you wait to leave, the harder it gets. In other words, once you complete your education, it will be easier to leave, take the "bull by the horn" and return to Nigeria to work to establish yourself. It may interest people to know that our plan did not work because we wanted to have "enough money" to last us a reasonable amount of time once we got back to Nigeria. But how much money was enough, when all the money went into the system, and we were only able to pay our bills with the meager amount left at the end of the month? We struggled month after month until time caught up with us, the children grew up in America. Other limiting factors made it extremely difficult for us to fulfill that wish. Maybe others will beat us in that effort.

Nigeria needs to return to the vibrant country it used to be, with rich heritage, many resources, friendly culture and welcoming spirit. Corruption has engulfed the whole country, making it a dangerous endeavor to go to the home of our birth. Those in power or high offices are obstacles to change. A lot of Nigerians are in the diaspora building up talents and working hard in building other nations. They are doctors, nurses, engineers, pharmacists, artists, lawyers, entrepreneurs, administrators, etcetera. Nigerians in the diaspora are making Nigeria proud by their achievements in academia and other fields. Yet the corruption in Nigeria has tarnished her image. Take for example, Nigerians are named as one of the highly educated people in America. Nigeria is blessed with multiple natural resources. These talents developed in the diaspora could be brought back to Nigeria to develop her natural resources and build her up to become one of the greatest countries in the world.

But alas! Is Nigeria at the point of no return? Fifty plus years after the Nigerian civil war, Nigeria is still struggling with widespread corruption. The youths cannot find jobs after graduating from university. Those working are not paid months after months. The youths will rather go to other countries than stay in Nigeria and work. Nigeria continues to lose the better part of her workforce. No one prefers staying in a foreign land forever if the conditions at home are favorable. There is fear and apprehension among most people in diaspora that coming home for good may not happen in their lifetime.

Some of the meetings of the Igbo indigens in America has become forums where these concerns are expressed. Suggestions about what to do to help improve things in Nigeria are never in short supply. Most of those are targeted to palliation, and relieving community sufferings. Widespread development can only be made possible from the people on top. But those on the top are just there for their own self interests. Instead, things are getting worse by the day.

In one of the meetings of the Igbos I attended some time ago, one man once said out of frustration, "Most people in the diaspora may be going home in boxes if Nigeria does not improve." I pray to counter that man's prediction. My people say in prayer, "Ukwu onye jiri ga ije ka oga eji ala." Translated, "the feet with which a traveler used to travel will be the same feet with which he will return". Not returning in a box! May that man's prediction never come true in Jesus Name...Amen.

For those aspiring to leave Nigeria, bear in mind that if Nigeria continues to remain in the ruts of corruption which have cut deep into the fabric of her society, be prepared to stay in the diaspora and fall into the same predicament others find themselves. I am hanging unto hope that Nigeria will improve one day and be ready to welcome all her children and grandchildren scattered all over the world and pray to be alive to see it happen! So, it is for other people from other parts of the world.

Chapter 1

Coming to America

The year was 1981, January 17th to be exact, my husband and I landed in New York City at the John F. Kennedy (JFK) Airport. For me it was my first airplane ride and my first trip to America. My husband was going to school at the University of Baltimore in Baltimore Maryland, United States of America since spring of 1979. He returned to Nigeria for the Christmas holiday in 1980, so I had joined him after our wedding on the trip back to United States to continue his education. We had travelled by the Nigerian Airways and arrived at about eight o'clock in the morning. Before we disembarked the aircraft, I looked out of the window and saw the ground covered by the snow. Apparently, it had snowed the night before and about two feet or more of snow was on the ground. Everywhere was covered by the snow except the path cleared for the aircraft landing, take off and service vehicles. The snow covered a vast area of the airport, seemed to extend up to the horizon as though it had joined the sky. Nothing prepared me for the experience of the bitter cold weather common in North America during the winter months.

My husband told me it would be cold, but I had no concept of how cold it would be. Yes, I brought my sweater was what I told my husband…ha ha! I had the sweater on alright, a leather jacket on me, and gloves on my hands when we landed. However, those were not enough to control my cold. I was shivering. My husband also put his own coat on me without much difference. Despite my discomfort from the cold feeling, my mind was fixated on the pure white snow that covered the ground. *"Wow!"* I said to myself, *"even the ground is white in the white man's land."* It was spectacular! Prior to that time, the things I knew about snow was singing it in the Christmas hymn "see amid the winter's snow". My husband explained to me that snow only happened in the winter months and soon they would melt as the sun came up, and the warm weather was coming in about two months. I had no idea.

I recall the Nigerian Airway plane from Lagos to New York City arrived late. We had missed our connecting flight to Baltimore, our final destination, which was about another hour's flight from New York City. We were then told to stay on standby for another plane. It took a couple of hours before we boarded the other plane to Baltimore Washington (BWI) Airport. It was a small aircraft carrying about twenty passengers and was flying low. I was able to look out of the window and saw the beautifully snow-decorated trees and shrubs. It was amazing to behold such a beautiful sight. Six hours after we landed in JFK, we landed in BWI airport where my husband's friend was waiting to take us immediately to my husband's studio apartment in 828 Park Avenue in Baltimore.

I am a baby boomer, born and raised in Imo state of Nigeria, the Igbo speaking Eastern Nigeria. The Igbos are an ethnic group in the present-day Nigerian nation, whose homeland lies between the Rivers Niger and the Cross River. The Igbos are one of the three major ethnic groups in Nigeria. A good number of Igbo people also live in the west of the Niger River. The Igbos speak a common language, the Igbo language. Different towns speak slight variations of the language called dialects. But the language is generally understood regardless of which dialect it was spoken. I was fortunate to have hailed from a well to do family according to the Nigerian standard. Growing up, I had the opportunity to attend good schools throughout my primary and secondary school days.

I was more exposed to some of American society and culture through movies and music when I entered nursing school in 1974 to 1977 at the Mater Misericordiea School of Nursing Afikpo in then Imo State of Nigeria. In nursing school, Saturday nights were movie nights. Those western movies like Wizard of Oz and comedies like

MY AMERICAN ADVENTURE (2024)

Stafford and Sons, the Cosby shows were shown by the expatriates managing the nursing school at the time. Watching similar movies and comedies helped me create my own impression of what American Society was. Michael Jackson - the Jackson Five's, Diana Ross's music and others were most popular in the 1970's. As most people who grew up in Nigeria in the 70's might agree, the America seen in pictures in the movies and those in the music then was depicted as beautiful in the superlative. The impression was as written in the American constitution paraphrased: "The land of milk and honey, where everyone sat on a pedestal, no one went to bed hungry, everyone had roofs over their heads, everyone plucked money off trees. It was a utopia of a place where all who lived in it had certain unalienable rights that included life, liberty and pursuit of happiness." (I used my own verbiage to paraphrase here, ha ha!)

Needless to say, my perception and that of some other people in Nigeria about American society then, was that life was a "breeze" and there were no struggles to make it in life in America. Plucking money off of trees in America for some people in Nigeria then was not a metaphor, some people actually believed it. I remember my aunt telling me that the story was very convincing she wanted to believe that the mighty dollar could be growing on trees... ha ha. When she, my aunt first came to America, she asked about the trees she heard were growing dollars. I told her I would show her the trees that grew the dollars so she could pluck hers… ha ha! Those dollar trees were the hospitals, the nursing homes, the restaurants, schools, home cleaning, landscaping, taxi driving... etcetera. The reality was she would need to struggle first to be qualified to do any of those, then go into one of those establishments and labor for forty hours a week to pluck the dollar equivalent of one week's job. Those descriptions of American society were not altogether true. Alas! Was I wrong? Yet, after I went through "hell" to make it in America, I am grateful it was all worth it.

Prior to coming to America, I heard nothing about the challenges that existed and still exist today in mainstream American society. On spending a short time after landing on American soil, it became apparent to me that the America I saw in pictures then was not exactly what was. I did not expect to see people stopping other people on the streets begging for quarter for coffee. Neither did I envision homeless people with their meager property living under the bridges and some living in street corners. I did not expect to learn that some people are so poor they could not afford decent housing and so, live in a place called "ghetto", including racial disparities and all the other maladies indigent in the mainstream American Society.

I never saw or imagined when I watched those movies when I was in Nigeria, that there could be dilapidated neighborhoods as prevalent in West and East of Baltimore city. I learned that those cities like New York City which appeared so much in many of the pictures shown outside USA, confused people like me and others into believing the whole of America was like that. New York, at its core was Manhattan, which was a densely populated and the world's major commercial, financial and cultural center featured a lot. It had all the "bells and whistles of the shinning city on the hill". Las Vegas with its iconic buildings and skyscrapers, and other American big cities like those, dominated the optics of the viewer living outside America. It was not surprising then that people would assume that the whole America was "heaven on earth" in the eyes of other people of the world. Anyone from outside the USA who has come to "see" the true America, can rightly say it is an irony that America is also riddled with some of those social maladies that were common in other parts of the world.

Most of the people I knew who emigrated from Nigeria in the 70's and 80's did so in search of quality education, and for better opportunities in life. This search was fueled by the aftermath of the Nigeria's three-year civil war, from 1967 to 1970. Education in Nigeria was one of the casualties of the civil war. The educational system in Nigeria, which was one of the best in Africa, crumbled as soon as the war was over. Most schools – universities, secondary and primary were destroyed beyond repair. The integrity of the West African Examination Council (WAEC) was most of the time compromised. (WAEC is the equivalent of high school graduation examination.) Widespread cheating in the WAEC exam became commonplace branded "expo 70". It was purported then that the WAEC exam questions were sold by the WAEC officials, and so anyone who could buy the exam questions could pass the WAEC exams easily. It was also believed then that people could write the exam without having been to high school or bought friends to take the exams for them.

That compromise of the integrity of the WAEC examination caused many Nigerians to lose faith in the educational system and the WAEC examinations. Parents and family members who could afford to send their children or relatives abroad to study did so in hopes of better education. In addition to obtaining quality education, it was believed that one is more exposed to better opportunities in life by studying abroad. Studying abroad and returning to Nigeria with higher degrees were also believed to accelerate one's opportunity to rising up to top levels in government or corporate world. My husband came to the United States in 1979 for the same reason. After completing one year at the university of Baltimore, my husband returned to Nigeria for Christmas holiday in 1980.

Our wedding took place on January 4th, 1981, after which we set off for the United States on January 16th. For me, I had no desire to go abroad initially. I had my nursing and midwifery degrees, took a job at the Holy Rosary Hospital Emekukwu in the midwifery school, teaching and making decent income. I thought it wise to stay behind and let my husband return to USA alone to complete his education while I continued working to establish us in Nigeria. But my husband insisted I joined him on his return to USA.

I considered that journey a trip for our honeymoon at the time, due to the fact that we left soon after our wedding. I did not prepare myself to stay long in America. As a matter of fact, I did not resign from my job, instead I request three month's leave hoping to come back to my job in about four months. I had just paid a one-year rent for my small apartment in Emekukwu near the hospital. My family had to retrieve my belongings when the rent was due again in 1981, at which time it became apparent I was not coming back any time soon.

The Harsh Reality

Coming to America then was a trip of adventure and curiosity for me. I wanted to use the opportunity to expose myself to other cultures of the world and gain knowledge I would otherwise not have gained should I remain in Nigeria. I wanted to experience all those things that made America the greatest country in the world. Then it was believed in Nigeria, made in America products or goods were the highest quality and highly sought after. Even now that China has flooded Nigerian markets with poor quality goods, American products still reign. I wanted to get clothes, shoes, jewelry, handbags, accessories and other belongings made in America. I wanted to shop, shop and shop to acquire the most beautiful things before returning to Nigeria.

I planned to spend a few months in America and enjoy all the things that made America "great". I wanted to tour important places in America and possibly visit many of the states. I wanted to develop a network of American friends that would be helpful to me in future visits. I thought that visit would open doors for my family to make future adventures or maybe useful to our children's education when we had them. Here we are, over four decades later, the dream of returning to Nigeria before retirement years hit, seems to be farfetched and disenchanting. When will it be possible for the sojourner to return home for good? Is my destiny to remain in a foreign land where I have now become a citizen?

An immigrant who lived in a warm climate like Nigeria, could not have come to America at the worst possible time of the year. January 17th 1981, was extremely cold in my opinion, with bone chilling temperatures in the 20 degrees Fahrenheit, and up to two feet of snow on the ground. Even the heat in the apartment was not enough to keep me warm. But the piles of snow on the ground was fascinating to see…mountains of snow everywhere. I was filled with awe at my new environment, the tall buildings, the beautiful scenery and the organized symphony of the traffic flow on the streets were awesome. It did not take me long to realize the lifestyle in America was completely different than what I was used to. My welcome to America! The snow I admired so much dissolved in a couple of days, flooding the streets and exposing the ground. "The land is not so white in the white man's land after all", just the same dirt land as it is in Nigeria.

Where Am I

I became curious about my environment. I needed to find out how to get around. Where would I go shopping for food, household goods and where to go to church were important to me. Our studio apartment was located near the Washington monument in Mount Vernon area. The monument was about one hundred and seventy-eight-feet tall, two hundred and twenty-eight steps to get to the top and sitting at the center of Charles' Street in Mount Vernon. Charles' Street splits to run on both sides of the Monument going one way in the northerly direction. It was built in honor of the first President of the United States, President George Washington. It was a beautiful monument to behold. It had a gothic appearance and nice pavements to sit and enjoy the evening sun. There was also a museum at the lower level which I loved to visit.

The next street over on Cathedral street was the Art Museum which was a tourist attraction. The art museum had arts from all over the world. I was mesmerized by the beautiful arts there the day I first visited it. The best thing about the museum was it was free to visit at first. Later there was a charge to visit. There was also the Baltimore Symphony Orchestra (BSO) on Park Avenue, just one block down the road from where we lived. I loved to watch the opera when they were in session. University of Baltimore was adjacent to the BSO, where my husband was going to school, a short walk from where we lived. Another street behind us was Howard Street, the home of Maryland General Hospital. Should I get sick, the hospital was one block behind me. The same Howard Street was the bus route to the Lexington Mall where I frequently visited for buying mostly food items.

On Cathedral Street, we found The Basilica of the National Shrine of the Assumption of the Blessed Virgin Mary. I learned the rich history of the cathedral as the first Roman Catholic Cathedral built in the United States of America and was among the first major religious buildings constructed in the nation after the adoption of the US constitution. How cool was that? That cathedral was where we went to Sunday services as we were both Catholics. The cathedral was eight blocks from our apartment, so convenient to either walk or jump into the bus. When I first walked into the cathedral, I could feel the magnificence and elegance of the church. It felt like God was really present! You could not help but walk into the church in reverence. I felt like my prayers were going directly to God when in that church.

For shopping, my husband told me about Lexington Market. Baltimore Lexington Market was said to be the oldest market in America, founded in the year 1782. That was where we purchased fresh fruits, vegetables, poultry and fish. It had and still has open stalls like our markets in Nigeria. I became very fond of visiting the Lexington Market as it reminded me of home. The market has remained the same way 'till today. Most recently, it has fallen into disrepute due to drug markets around it making it a dangerous place to go. Current news reports indicate that the Baltimore City officials have taken note of the drug activities around and in the market. At the time of writing this book, there were talks about tearing it down, driving away the drug dealers and rebuilding it. There was also the old town mall on the east side of the town that we seldom visited.

Baltimore Inner Harbor was and still is a tourist spot. It provided me with exciting place to visit on the weekends. In the heart of downtown Baltimore, I loved it. It had everything from scenic waterfront and spectacular museums to children's playground and carousels. There were mighty ships docked along the edges of the harbor. First time I saw a ship live other than in pictures. I was mesmerized by the size of the ships. People were getting in and out of the ships for excursions. I dared not go in because I did not like to go close to a large body of water.

Maryland Science Center showcasing exhibitions and demonstrations of science, the solar system and more, sat on the south end of the harbor.

Across from the science center stood the mighty aquarium with beautiful and exotic fishes in display. There were people riding the water taxis 'till the boat disappeared into the horizon. There were many shops where products and arts from different parts of the world were displayed and sold. It had a beautiful promenade to take a nice stroll. Should I talk about the restaurants? Seafood galore all around. I loved Phillips' Seafood, Rusty Scupper and the others. The Inner Harbor had this exquisite charm that branded Baltimore the charm city. It was about a ten-minute bus ride from our apartment, so convenient to visit. First time I visited Inner Harbor, I felt like staying there all day to feast my eyes.

The charm city had a lot more perks to love. The authentic crab cake, the fried liver and gizzard at the Lexington market, and the fried lake trout were my favorites. The University of Maryland hospital was down the street from the harbor. Johns Hopkins University Hospital on the east side of town, the beautiful federal hill neighborhood on the south end, and University of Baltimore on the north side. All those universities and their hospitals attracted an array of students from multiple nations. It was not difficult to meet other students from various parts of the world. All these things, places and others I was yet to discover made me feel like Baltimore would be a nice place to be until I heard not so great stories about Baltimore.

Baltimore like other USA cities had some ills that no one could be proud of. I learned there were some areas of the city never to venture out to especially in the night, mainly west and east sides of the city. That is where the ghettos who are poverty-stricken people lived. The area was infested by rodents and roaches, and has boarded crumbling homes and drug ridden neighborhoods creating dangerous streets. Young people are carrying guns and shooting at each other. I heard about killings in the streets of Baltimore. Every day there were news reports recounting the number of people killed the night before, by gangs and drug dealers fighting for drug market territories. I was scared to go out on the streets for fear of being shot. I heard about racial discrimination and bigotry, which I was yet to experience in a big way.

The long-established institutions like Johns Hopkins University and Hospital, University of Maryland and Hospital,

MY AMERICAN ADVENTURE (2024)

University of Baltimore, the Baltimore Symphony Orchestra and other nicer neighborhoods attracted college students, graduates and entrepreneurs making up for what Baltimore lacked.

I was warned to never go out in the night to those dangerous areas of the city. As someone new in America, all those warnings greatly limited my movement. Not knowing where the safer areas were, I was afraid to go outside the areas I had gone to with my husband. But I was curious to know more about my new town. I had to depend on other people to help me navigate the city and the system. I had not met any friends of my own. My husband's friends, all males were the only people I knew at the time. So far, the only person who could help me was my husband, but he was in school during the day and worked in the evening. I could not go out much until he was free, mainly on the weekends when he was off. Television set became my companion in the daytime. I watched almost every program that came up...news reports, soap operas, game shows, comedy, you name it, I watched it. I knew all of the programs by name, the characters that played and the time they aired.

As women, we treasure getting our hair done periodically. In Nigeria, I visited the hair salon once a month. I came to America with shoulder length fully relaxed hair. One of my most important need during the first couple of months was to find a good hair salon. I did not have a female friend who could direct me in that "department". Most of my husband's friends were male students and were no help to me in that area. My husband had a barber, I could have gone there to get my hair all cut off but I decided to do it myself.

Doing it myself was a big mistake. I had no experience in using relaxer or its application. All I did then was sat on the beautician's chair, and in about two hours, I paid her and left. The first time I applied the relaxer to my hair, my hair started shedding within two weeks. Oh God! I had ruined my hair. I had very nice patches of hair all over my head. Long story short, I ended up at the barber shop and had my hair all cut off. I could have had a nicer cut if I had just had it cut before I ruined it. It was cut so low that it took time to regrow. That is what my people call "penny wise pound foolish". I learned never to fool with chemicals to my hair again.

Chapter 2

The Cultural Shock

As a new Immigrant in the United States in the early 80's, one was made to believe that America was a place where one could live life, pursue one's goals and dreams unburdened by fear or intimidation. America was a place where traditional work ethics centered on hard work paid great dividends. I quickly realized the opportunities available for everyone to grab. I believed and still believe all those were true. However, there were social ills and culture in America which were shocking to me!

"How can anyone be homeless in America? Did that person drop out of the sky?" I asked. Does it mean that the person has no relatives or friends he or she could squat with 'till he or she got his or herself together, as was customary where I came from? It was not long before the true American society began to unravel before me. Soon, I would be in the thick and thin of American society, and have a clear view of who they really are and what they are made of.

Just like any other nation, America has its own share of the social ills that were rampant elsewhere in the world. As I was hunkering down at home due to the cold weather, most of the time I tuned up my "companion", the television, to ABC news which was my favorite channel in the mornings. I watched the morning news, twelve o'clock news and the 6 o'clock evening news.

One day, I was listening to a news report. There came a story about one of the subsidized housing (which they called project) communities in Baltimore where residents lived in a substandard condition. The managers allegedly neglected repairs in the homes and the buildings became dilapidated. Pictures of homes that had suffered serious neglects were in display. One lady invited news media to her home to show broken windows, peeling wall papers and paints, bathroom tubs that had literally separated from the wall, molds everywhere. The lady said she has been begging for repairs for over a year.

Rats and mice were roaming wildly in the area, courageously standing on the streets waving at people passing by.... literally! Thrash littered on the streets leading to and all around that community. There were open drug markets day or night, and shootings were rampant. The pictures were unbelievable, so gross like, or even worse than what could be seen in some parts of Ajegule in Lagos, Nigeria. It was also reported that some residents would rather live on the streets than live in any of the buildings in that community. It was unbelievable. There was allegation too that the managers would demand sexual favors before they would do repairs in some homes occupied by females. I asked, *"Is this America?"*

Within a few days, I got out for my first shopping trip at the Lexington market which was about a ten-minute bus ride. My means of transportation at the time was the bus. My husband and I were travelling together. When we reached Lexington and got off the bus, lo! and behold a man dressed in ragged clothes and coat was sitting at the street corner. The man had a plastic cup which he was waving in front of people passing by.

"Can I have a quarter for coffee" he said.

I immediately thought the man was crazy. I was quickly corrected by my husband saying the man was homeless not mentally ill. I could not believe anyone in America could be homeless and look like that man until I saw him. I remembered the pictures of America I had in mind, the "shinning city on the hill". How could anybody look this wretched in America? Is this truly America?

With the weather getting warmer, I began to venture out more, mostly to the grocery stores. Soon, I began to learn the American way of life. At the time, I called America the land of anonymity. It is important to mention here that these were my observations at the time, and other immigrants may not have had the same experience that led me to believe America was a land of anonymity. We lived in an apartment building and never knew who our neighbors were until we moved from that apartment building. Where I came from, people were sociable and knew everybody that lived in the same compound or even in the same villages. I say that because after I have been in that apartment building for about two months, I became curious about who our next-door neighbors were.

There were always loud noises coming from the apartment to the left of us, so I was sure people lived there. I was simply looking for someone close to my apartment who I could befriend to help me navigate my new environment. As said earlier, my husband was too busy to help. I knocked on the door. I could tell someone peeped through the peephole and never opened the door. I knocked again but there was no response. I knew there were people in that apartment because I just heard voices too, but why did they not open the door? Baffled me. *"Is this how people in America behave?"* I asked. I was not able to find a friend in our apartment building 'till we left.

I was cautioned never to do such a thing again, because I could be accused of being an intruder and potentially endanger my life. If they were nefarious people, I could be harmed. That was mind boggling to me. I also noticed that on the streets, people would not greet or answer the greetings of anyone they don't know or a stranger. I would greet people I met on the street, especially those I considered older than me. My culture demands you greet your elders regardless of whether you know them or not.

I noticed that sometimes greeting unfamiliar people on the streets brought an ugly stare to the greeter. I observed that people viewed strangers with suspicion until they got to know them. People addressed each other by first names not minding the age. Back home in Nigeria, older people were addressed as Mr. or Mrs. I was surprised older people would even ask to be addressed by their first names, and not minding their age and the respect age accorded them. In those days in Nigeria, people took offense if not properly addressed with their title: Mr. Mrs., Chief, Doctor. Etc. Most Nigerians, even those in the diaspora embrace that culture 'till today. I also noticed everyone seemed to be in a rush a lot of times.

Our First Dwelling

We lived on the third floor in what was called a studio apartment. The apartment was one big open room with no partitions. Our bed was on one corner of the room, one sofa on another side. The kitchen on the third side and the bathroom in one corner. Thank God the bathroom was enclosed and with a door. We sat the TV on a small table in the center of the room facing the sofa. There was a space at the head of the bed that we used as closet. Coming from a place where homes and rooms were generally large, that whole apartment could be a bedroom only. I was extremely uncomfortable staying there. When my husband's friends stopped by, I felt so embarrassed for lack of privacy. Even if I was tired and wanted to lay down and relax, I was forced to stay up until his friends left.

In addition to lack of privacy, the apartment had cockroach infestation. Yak! Those were the baby cockroaches which the Americans called roaches. They were disgusting! I did not see those baby cockroaches when I was in Nigeria. Nigeria had the bigger cockroaches which were usually found in unkempt homes or storage places like warehouses. They were never common in clean homes to my knowledge, as they were in America. Outside there were rodents running around the thrash dump area. Thank God I did not see them inside the building! I began to think the whole America was like that. Where was the "shinning city on the hill" I saw when I was in Nigeria? It just happened that I had not been able to go out yet was my thought.

The only thing I liked about the apartment was the only window that was looking out to the main street - Park Avenue, which was a one-way street in the northbound direction. I used to stay on the bed and watched the street from the window. There was one traffic light right in front of our building. I liked to watch the flow of cars, and people walking up and down the street. Pedestrians were walking like everyone was in a hurry. There were people on scooters zooming through traffic. Bicyclers also sharing the road with cars. (They would be knocked down if they ventured that in Nigeria.) Cars obeyed traffic signals consistently which was not always so in Nigeria.

The condition I found our apartment was so deplorable to me. The roaches gave me nightmares! I was not able to sleep well at night for fear the roaches could crawl on me. I wanted to leave there so bad, but my husband still had a lease which had two months left on it. The apartment managers would spray insecticides, but that kept them away for about a week, then they came back. We started looking for another apartment and about three months later, we moved to 1208 North Calvert Street which was a one-bedroom apartment. The apartment was still within the area and in a better condition. Everywhere I was used to going were still close by on the bus or cab. The rooms were big and had no roaches. I had privacy I greatly yearned for.

Watching TV gave me so much joy. My favorite morning show was the "Price Is Right" hosted by Bob Barker. I would also watch the twelve-noon news, later, the soap opera... All My Children, One Life To Live, General Hospital and Dynasty on the weekdays. On Saturdays, sports came on TV. I would watch basketball and soccer, which we called football in Nigeria. When American football came up on TV, I did not understand it. All I saw were players wearing the helmet like astronauts going into space! The players would line up and opposing teams put their heads together, then scattered, and chased each other around. Sometimes they would tackle each other, or one guy would knock down the other. I saw one guy lifted a big guy and threw him on the ground, ouch! Sometimes they knocked their heads together with the cracking sound of the helmet. I saw one guy being carried out on a stretcher with injury, the other limping away to the sideline.

I thought American football was a rough game. I was amazed at how so many people liked the game. I did not understand the game or how watching such a game would be entertaining to so many people.

MY AMERICAN ADVENTURE (2024)

A game that would cause serious injury such as head injury, fractures and many other injuries would be so revered in America? Why would anyone play this game in the first place, knowing how dangerous it was? I would change the channel immediately. I found no interest in watching the game I called "American football". Little did I know that game played by Americans which I branded "American football" would open the doors wide for my children's success in life. Was football the key to opening mine and my children's destiny?

It was initially difficult to understand the American English accent. Having studied English as it was taught in Nigeria during the colonial days by the British, I was confident I was in total command of English language when I came to America. Though Nigeria has over two hundred ethnic languages, English was, and still is the common language used to get around the country and teach in schools. However, it was difficult at first to understand the English language spoken by Americans, especially the illiterate ones. It appeared they substitute the letter T in words with D or sometimes R. For example, the Americans call Rita, my name sounding like Reader. At first, I never knew that was how they called my name.

Once, I was in the antenatal clinic waiting room to see the obstetrician. When it was my turn to see the doctor, I heard what sounded like "Miss Reader" being called. I did not realize it was my name that was called so I did not respond. My record was marked as "did not answer". When I noticed people that came after me were called, I went to inquire why my name was not called. That was how I got to learn my name was "Reader" according to the American accent. At the same time, some Americans accuse people from other countries whose primary language was not English, as having an accent, while their own accent was more difficult to understand.

The people we exchanged visits with then were fellow foreign students. Slowly we began to also associate with other students of American origin. One day, I attended a graduation party with my husband for one of my husband's friends. My husband's friend was from Baltimore (Baltimorean as they called them). That was the place I first noticed that women did smoke in this country. Most of the young ladies had cigarettes and smoking with the men. Some girls were dressed provocatively, chasing the men and kissing them openly without bashfulness! That kind of behavior was abhorred in Nigeria when I was there, except if the person the girl was kissing was her husband. Even at that, they did not kiss in public.

Our apartment was across from the Waxter Center for Senior Citizens on Park Avenue. The center had tree-lined walkways with benches placed under the trees, where people sat to enjoy the evening breeze or sunshine. One day it was around twelve noon. I looked out of the window and saw two men on the bench kissing and doing their "thing". I was flabbergasted. *"Whaaaat!"* I screamed. In the broad daylight? *"My eyes have seen my ears!"* No one can see their own ear without a mirror of course. But my people say that when someone saw something they considered an abominable act. This is America!

These early experiences and many others I witnessed or heard about, taught me that I am not living in a utopia of a place. Soon, I began to learn about other maladies rampant in most neighborhoods: drug use and abuse, addictions, unemployment, teenage pregnancy, crimes riddled cities, illiteracy, school dropouts, elder abuse and abandonment, gangs, killings on the streets of Baltimore, people being alienated from their families and the likes. I again remembered the stories I heard about America when I was in Nigeria… America the utopia of a place, "the shinning city on the hill".

Grocery stores were my favorite places to visit. I visited Acme store on the next street from ours very often. First time I bought fruits: banana, oranges, apples and ground nuts (peanuts) plus other food items. The fruits and groundnuts were very plump but tasted "watered down". They did not have the kind of sweetness the ones at home in Nigeria had. I came to learn they were grown with fertilizers and pesticides. The foods we ate were mostly hamburger, French fries, hot dogs, rice, beans, spaghetti and mac/cheese. Needless to say, the pounds started piling up on me! Within the first three months, I packed up thirteen pounds…Ouch. At that time there were no African markets around to buy African food. The closest we could get was Asian markets, but those Asian markets did not sell most of the foods or ingredients and spices we needed to make our favorite authentic

Nigerian dishes such as soup and foofoo. All the ingredients I came with had exhausted.

After eating spaghetti and macaroni, rice and beans to ad nauseum, I began experimenting to make Nigerian food such as soup and foofoo. Soup without real crayfish, mangala fish or stock fish did not taste the same. The chicken was too soft, soggy and required a lot of spices to make it palatable. Back home the chicken was raised without fertilizers or artificial feed. They were skinny and had a natural delicious taste. I did not like the taste of the soft chicken. There was no gari to make the foofoo. However, I was incredibly innovative in having found that foofoo could be made with pancake mix which turned out very well. We used pancake mix for foofoo until years later when African markets started popping up all around, at which time we were able to get ingredients to make our authentic Nigerian meals.

My favorite clothing stores were Hecht's and Hustlers both on Howard street in Baltimore. Those were middle to high end clothing stores. I could easily find clothes tailored to my size and in my styles. I was highly elated when I found out that one could return the clothes within a specified period of time and receive one's money back if they changed their mind. Such never happened in Nigeria when I was there. Once you left the store with the merchandise, regardless of whether you left the store for one minute before you changed your mind, the merchandise was yours. One would never get one's money back. That was a general unwritten rule. So, you must be SURE you really want the item before paying for it.

I would pack up so many beautiful clothes and saved them for my going back to Nigeria. Epstein on the same area was where I purchased household goods. As I was not working at the time, those were the stores I hung out on regular bases, whether I needed anything or not. I spent a lot of time at the Lexington market, binging on the fried liver and the giblets. Some days I jumped into the bus to Lexington mall just to do window shopping. That was how I occupied my spare time to avoid boredom. Sometimes there were artists performing or band playing on the stage at the market to entertain people. I would hang around to enjoy whatever entertainment was going on.

First Tastes of Prejudice

Three months later, around March 1981, I got tired of staying indoors and the weather had become tolerable. Having lived a highly active life in Nigeria, I got really bored staying idle. I began looking for a job but could not be hired as a nurse because I had not taken the Maryland Nursing board exam. I needed a Registered Nurse (RN) license to work in America. I had sent in my application to the Maryland Board of Nursing, but the board was waiting for my credentials from Nigeria in order to approve and schedule me for the board exam.

While waiting, I got a job at a nursing home near my apartment, Pennsylvania Avenue Nursing Home. Mrs. Burns was the director of the nursing home at the time. She had special affinity to the African Nations and so, was very welcoming of me when she found out I was from Nigeria. She told me stories of some African countries she visited: South Africa, and Ghana. She hired me the same day with a starting salary of $2.85/hour. She said once I passed the board exam, my salary would go up. I knew I was taken advantage of for not being paid more as a skilled nurse, but I was happy to work and make some money. The nursing home was a walking distance from where I lived therefore, there was no expense at commuting. My weekly pay was close to $98.0 after taxes. It was enough to augment my husband's salary to pay our bills.

Working in that Nursing home exposed me to the real American people... White and Black. It was a 40-bed nursing home on two levels of the building. Only one registered nurse stayed on duty each shift managing the two floors. Most of other staff were either Certified Nurse Assistants (CNAs) or Licensed Practical Nurses (LPNs). It was then that I first had a taste of prejudice in the workplace! Not long, I would face discrimination against foreign born which was rampant among Americans, be it white or black people. License Practical Nurses and the Certified Nursing Assistants did the hands-on patient care, and the RN did more management of the units. I was hired to do wound care throughout the building.

When the CNA's found out that I was a Registered Nurse from my country, they started thumping noses at me. I could see they were jealous of me. They could not understand why my only job was to do wound care throughout the nursing home patient care areas…the two floors. In any given day, I would do up to ten to twelve wound cares. Most of the CNAs had no understanding of how much work doing wound care in the whole building was. They did not believe I had enough work to do. Sometimes the brave ones among them would approach me to demand I helped them with patient care, just to pick a fight with me, though they were told numerous times by the supervisor not to bother me. Their hate and disgust of me were palpable because they had no power to force me to do hands-on patient care with them. Most of those CNA's and the LPNs who were antagonistic to me were black people.

It was difficult to carry on conversation with them because of their numerous slang words and the use of curse words. Say for example, instead of saying "I am not doing it" Americans said "a ain't gonna do it", or "e ein't my problem" which means it is not my problem. With time, I began to understand their language and followed their conversations but could not speak like them. Sometimes it appeared they did not understand good English, or they pretended they did not understand when I spoke. They would ask "Watch you say?" instead of "What did you say?". They had so many different clicks which at times made it difficult to relate to them. The nursing assistants were very prejudiced to the point that their actions were very perceptible even when they said nothing. I got ganged up on a lot. Only one LPN was approachable and so I tried to befriend her. Her name was Sharon.

As one who recently immigrated to a new country, the way things were done was different from how I learned it, even in the health care system. I had to learn new ways of carrying out nursing duties. Sharon was the only one who helped me navigate the nursing home culture. She came to my aid when I got the attacks from the nurse assistants. At lunch time, she went with me to buy lunch, and we sat together to eat in the nursing home dining room. On the days she was off, I sat alone as the other staff avoided me like I had leprosy. The treatment they meted to me one day, made me learn a lesson never to join any of them for lunch anymore. I was very shocked that people would treat other people with such cruelty.

That day, a group of the staff were eating on one table. There was more room on that table to accommodate more people. The moment I sat down with my lunch on an open space on that table, all the staff carried their food and moved to another table....in unison. Initially I thought that something was wrong with the table we were sitting on, so I followed them to the next table. One girl yelled at me "are you blind... bitch?" and they all moved again to another table. The rest of the ladies laughed out loud. I did not know they moved from that table in order to avoid me.

They were avoiding me as if I had a plague. I felt so embarrassed! There were patients' families visiting with their loved ones sitting at other tables. They saw it all! All eyes were on me. I lost my appetite and packed up my lunch then left the dining room. It was appalling to know people could be treated with such an undignified way in this great country called America. Where I came from, people were, and still are welcomed especially those from foreign lands. That was my first time hearing the word... bitch. I did not know the meaning at the time, but I knew it was something bad, a word I learned later should not be said openly, let alone address somebody like me with it.

I tried so hard to make another friend in that nursing home, but it was not possible. Everything I did for them to accept me did not work. Instead, I infuriated them more. Every day I worked, it appeared a "trap" was set to get me by any one of them. Predictably, I always fell into somebody's trap, either by being asked for instance, to help lift a patient or feed a patient which they knew I was not supposed to be doing. "Well, she is a staff here, she should help with patient care", they always reported me to the supervisor. The supervisor would again remind them that Rita was not a CNA or LPN. I worked there for a couple of months and got tired of the "drama". Sadly, this kind of prejudice was not peculiar to this nursing home. I am sad to say I endured similar treatments at some other places I worked during the early part of my life in America 'till later in my sojourn when I learned how to navigate the American society. This is America?

Learning the hard way

I did not know that petty stealing was common at that nursing home. I learned it happened in other places too. One day, I had gone to work with $10 in my coat pocket. That was the money I allotted for my lunch that week. I did not have my own locker, so I hung my coat on an open hanger in the locker room. Come lunch time, I grabbed my coat and went to the nearest McDonald with my friend Sharon, not knowing the money in my coat pocket had been stolen. I ordered hamburger, French fries and coke which were mostly the food I knew at the time. When it was time to pay, I dipped my hand into my coat pocket. Lo! and behold, the money was gone.

I was very embarrassed! I knew I had put the money in my coat pocket that morning as I was preparing to go to work. What could have happened to it? Did it fall out of my pocket on my way to work and I did not know it? I was unable to pay for my lunch that day. The most embarrassing part of the ordeal was telling the cashier to cancel my order because I could not find my money. I reported it to Sharon that I was sure I put the ten dollars in my pocket that morning. When she realized I had hung my coat on an open hanger, Sharon said to me, "Your money had been stolen." Sharon told me never to leave any valuables in the locker room unless there was a lock, because the item would be stolen. She paid for my lunch that day and I paid her back the next day.

I learned the hard way that I needed to always protect my belongings. I needed my own locker, at the time I did not have any. Sharon helped me get a locker to secure my belongings. According to Sharon, my coat would have been the next that would be taken, if I did not secure it. That was an eye opener to me. So, there was petty stealing in America. Petty stealing was uncommon in a place like the nursing home when I was in Nigeria. Pick pockets could happen in open markets but not in a decent facility like the nursing home. I did not expect petty stealing to be common in mainstream America. Why would it be, where everyone was well off and sitting on the proverbial "pedestal"? This is America.

The Biggest Cultural Shock of All For Me

What shocked me the most was teenage pregnancy and how acceptable or tolerable it appeared to be in the American society. My first day in the antenatal clinic, I saw young pregnant girls, the youngest said she was thirteen years old, also there for antenatal care. There were four of them and all were black girls. They sat close to one another in the doctor's waiting room as though they knew each other. I was also sitting close to them. I was wondering whether those children were married that young? How come they were pregnant at that age?

I listened to their conversation and one of them said to the others, her mother was very happy she got pregnant because that would mean getting more money. Another girl, a little older…maybe seventeen or eighteen, said she was on her second pregnancy. She did get more money when she had her first baby, so she went for the second. I was flabbergasted! So those children were pregnant and not married! Incredible! I thought to myself, *"Who paid children to get pregnant in America? Is there an adoption agency paying teenagers to get pregnant?"* Whoa, I thought I had seen and heard it all!!

In Nigeria where I came from, being pregnant and not married brought enormous shame to the girl and her family. The girl would not even appear in public let alone brag about being pregnant. Most parents would send their unmarried pregnant daughter away in secret, until the baby got born. Unmarried and becoming pregnant leaves a stigma on the girl and the family forever. The girl most of the time would no longer be able to get a good husband if she decided to be married in the future. The community would brand her "damaged good". If the girl ever got married, she would be lucky to be a second or third wife. That stigma may even affect other females born in that family. That explained the reason the parents sent the girl away as soon as they found out about the pregnancy… to minimize the effect the stigma would have on her family and female siblings.

Later, I learned that what those pregnant children were talking about was welfare payments. The more children they had, the more money they got in welfare payments. They got subsidized housing, Women, Infant and Children (WIC) nutrition program, so they had enough for their families. WIC offered mothers "resources, knowledge and tools to help you be the mom you want to be. It offered them healthy food, breast feeding support, and nutrition education" (adapted from WIC Nutrition Program – Women, Infants and Children at Maryland government website). That was what those kids were talking about!

Those children who were having children, they probably would not be able to care for, because they were paid money in welfare! What kind of care would a thirteen-year-old mother give to another child? Even with all the resources that were offered by the government, raising children is not only about providing food and shelter. Those were the children that did not go to school because they were having babies. Other children were in school and they were in the antenatal clinic. Those pregnant teens were not mature enough to develop the nurturing skills needed to care for a child. They probably depended on their parents to take care of their babies. That would be additional burden on their parents, some of whom may have been single mothers themselves living in poverty. Having children when they were children would multiply the poverty they were already living in and pass it on from one generation to the next.

Some of the CNAs working with me in the Nursing Home did the same when they were teens. Having children and not married was and still is an acceptable culture in America. Their attitudes and body language exhibited deep rooted anger they felt all the time. I always wondered why they were always looking mean and angry. I speculated it could be that they were angry at themselves. Some of them who had children as teenagers were probably looking back with regrets. It was commonly acceptable in the American society, so they had done it out of ignorance! And now they are regretting having done it.

But it was not too late to change the way their life was. They were mostly young women, many of them under twenty-five years of age. It was not too late to go back to school. The question was; would they be motivated and disciplined enough to go through with school? How did those children view marriage? Would they ever be married in their lifetime or remain single mothers? Does America value marriage?

While I was still working at the nursing home, I learned that drug abuse and alcoholism were very common in America. In addition to both men and women engaging in smoking of cigarettes, both also engaged in alcohol and drug abuse. Many a time as I walked to and from work, some of the victims of drug abuse were seen sleeping at street corners. I would hear gossips about some of the employees at the nursing home abusing alcohol or drugs. At that point, I had not learned much about how to spot drug users. Not until I went back to school did I learn about the disease. There was never a time I heard anything about drug abuse in Nigeria at the scope it was in America until I left Nigeria. However, I could easily spot the ones using alcohol because of the peculiar smell of alcohol around them.

One day, I learnt first-hand what a devastating effect using drugs could do to its victims. On that woeful day, a twenty-nine-year-old man working at the housekeeping department of the nursing home named Mr. Johnson had tumbled down a twenty-eight-step stairway and landed on the first floor head first. He suffered a massive head injury. An ambulance arrived within five minutes of his fall and whisked him away. I heard he later died at the hospital. There were gossips going around that he and some other men and women working with him in the housekeeping department constantly used drugs. There was report that earlier that day he was seen acting strange with stumbling walk. Someone could have saved his life if they had reported him to the manager at the time of those behaviors. But they did not because no one wanted to "snitch" on him… Now he is dead!

It is a well-known fact that drug abuse destroyed and still destroys many lives in America. I would learn that some Americans, adults, teenagers and youths indulge in drug use. Cocaine, marijuana and alcohol were the most frequently used drugs to help them experience euphoria which they constantly sought. In addition to the addicting effects, each and every one of those drugs have adverse health implications which affect those indulging in them. Overdose deaths were and still are common. Like in the case of Mr. Johnson, a lot of times, drug users suffer serious injuries when they are "high". They got involved in automobile accidents more frequently than the general public.

Their actions when they drink and drive, or "high" could be a death sentence for an innocent person who was engaging on personal business of their own. Or be a cause for an innocent person to have a devastating injury that would last them a lifetime. I learned that the drug users were big consumers of the health care system costing the country a lot of money and putting so much strain in the economy.

Not only the health issues, but drug use also destroyed families. I would learn that even some pregnant mothers used drugs throughout their pregnancy. They would have drug-addicted infants with numerous complications ranging from deformities to delayed development with lifelong medical issues. It was also quite common that such women might not have sought antenatal care during their pregnancy. It baffled me to know that people could put their unborn children through such situations. It seemed like they did not care what happened to the child they were carrying. That was in line with not being ready for motherhood for some of the girls. This is America, the shining city on the hill!

Chapter 3

Adjustment

No one nation is devoid of societal ills. As I would come to know, America is no exception. However, no matter their numerous problems, there were and still are a lot to be desirous of going to and living in America. I learned it was and still is possible to live in poverty or homeless in America and still survive. There were charity organizations that assisted people in need. There were food banks and soup kitchens for people who could not afford food, as long as they could get to the food center. There were government programs that cater for the underprivileged. Housing for the homeless to those who qualify, food stamps, unemployment income, low-income housing programs, veteran assistance programs, elderly and disabled programs… the list is endless. Primary school education was free and college tuition was discounted for the indigens. Medical care was free for some eligible members of the community, to name a few.

Some of these programs were not available in Nigeria during my time there. Everyone worked hard to earn a living and the less privileged depended on family or friends for help. Even at that, no one was ever homeless to my knowledge when I was in Nigeria. It was considered a moral obligation for a member of a family who was better off. That person who was better off was expected to help the less privileged in his or her family. The stigma attached to the family of a homeless person was tremendous. Whatever the better off person in that family had, was used to care for all family members in need.

MY AMERICAN ADVENTURE (2024)

There was never a time he or she would say to a homeless family member "I don't have a place for you to sleep or I have no room in my house for you". Any space in the home could be turned into a sleeping space just to accommodate a homeless family member. That was how the people of Asian, Spanish or Mexican descents were and are still doing the same today. Unless that person had done something that could cause the rest of the family to ostracize him or her. That was why when I learned there were homeless people in America, it was mind boggling to me at first. As time went on, I came to understand the other deep-rooted issues that caused homelessness in America.

I was truly fortunate to have come to America with a nursing degree. In the early 80's there was severe shortage of Registered Nurses (RNs) in America. During those years, America was importing nurses from the Philippines and other parts of the world. Once I got my nursing license, it was not difficult to land a nursing job at the Rehabilitation Center in Baltimore. My starting salary was $12.00/hr. That was a huge jump from $2.86 an hour I was making when working in the nursing home.

In Nigeria during my time, the Registered Nurse (RN) played mostly managerial and educational roles. The RN was in-charge of ward management, rounding with the doctors, patient/family education, medication injections, wound care, instillations, oxygen administration, pill administration and all other skilled care. The family was taught by the RNs how to do baths, mouth care, incontinent care, feeding and turning patients in bed for those who could not turn themselves. When a patient got admitted, families must always provide a family member at the patient's bedside to do the physical care for the patient. The Ward Maids (equivalence of Certified Nursing Assistants) helped the family with the hands-on care. It was never my primary duty to do hands-on care of patients. I had mostly done management and teaching in the midwifery school prior to coming to the United States.

Adjustment was difficult because things were done differently. The patient's population was also different. The facility was part nursing home and part rehabilitation. I was in the nursing home section so most of the patients were total care. That meant they were completely dependent in others for doing all activities of daily living… bathing, clothing, shaving, feeding, and turning. A lot of them were incontinent and required frequent cleaning and changing of clothes and bedding. I was not used to doing total patient care prior to coming to America. In Nigeria, there were no Nursing homes at the time. Most patients in the hospitals were what we called "walky-talky" that did not require labor intensive efforts to take care of them. My speculation as to why those total care patients were not in Nigerian hospitals was people did not survive once they become completely incapacitated. Besides, I abhorred having to clean people's "behinds". As stated, as much as I loved and still love nursing, I never liked doing patient personal care. That was why I chose the administration and education in nursing path. The ward maids did the cleaning! That was one reason I had a hard time adjusting to my new job. In America, registered nurses do the cleaning too! I was hired for night shift and given a few days of RN orientation. Due to nursing shortage, even when I felt I needed longer orientation, I was released. A lot of times, on night shift, I was the only RN on duty on my unit. Luckily, other units had at least one RN on duty, so I did not have to cross cover to the other units.

    Being the only RN on duty in my unit, I was given the charge nurse role, which meant I was responsible for nursing assistants and LPNs. Nursing Assistants as noted before, were my adversaries when I worked in the previous nursing home. The rehab center also had predominantly nursing assistants, and some LPNs. It was deja-vous all over again! In addition, I was not confident of myself being in-charge of the unit with my limited work experience in America. I was always filled with apprehension that something could go wrong someday that might cause me to lose my nursing license. The thought of potentially loosing my nursing license caused a high level of anxiety because it had become existential for me in America at the time, to maintain active license. Losing my license would mean losing my job. That caused me to develop an anxiety disorder at the time which took a long time to go away.

    I did not trust my subordinates and felt they might purposefully set me up to fail or get me in serious trouble. The challenges I faced then were daunting, overwhelming and even exhausting. I was doing hands-on patient care which I was not used to doing; cleaning other peoples' behinds which I abhorred. At the same time in-charge of a group of rebellious subordinates. I would come home from work so exhausted. My back, my legs and arms hurting to the point I would weep. I wanted so bad to go back to Nigeria but not yet. I learned that as a woman of color as they called us, who was also an immigrant, I had three strikes against me. First, I was a woman, next a black woman, next an immigrant with accent. I was vulnerable to insults and badmouthing more from those people who looked exactly like me! But I did not understand why. Why would people I called my sisters hate me so much? It appeared to me that they were always looking for ways to bring me down. Most of those nursing assistants were as old as my mother. I learned that some of them have been working as nurse assistants for as many as thirty to forty years… even before I was born.

Some of them probably could do some of the RN jobs due to being exposed to them for a long time. But they did not have the license to perform any skilled care. Sometimes I would wonder to myself, why would anyone work in that lower level for that many years and never thought of going to school to upgrade their status in life? They had opportunities at their disposal, but they failed to grab it. Now they are jealous that a foreigner was more qualified than them due to being more educated. They thought RNs were doing skilled procedures which anyone who got trained could do. The difference is that the RN was trained in critical thinking to assess patients, develop care planning, execute the plans and evaluate them.

Those qualities, the CNAs did not have. It took up to four years in school of nursing to acquire those special skills that made one a registered nurse. How ignorant those CNAs could be! Being much younger than most of them, they were filled with resentment and indignation. "How can this little girl rule it over us", was the sentiment I sensed, sometimes expressed to my hearing. They showed much antagonism when close interaction occurred between me and them. I would hear comments like, "I can do your job." "Yee en nobody gonna tell me what to do" or "e'int got notin to do with me". It was always a tense working environment.

Some of them sometimes would refuse their assignments and abandon any patients they made up their minds not to take. Since it was night shift, there was no supervisor I could report them to till the next morning. Being responsible for the unit as the charge nurse, I would ensure whatever patient they abandoned got care from me. A lot of times, I would be behind in my own assignment trying to do my job and other people's jobs; the one who abandoned their job in protest for me being in-charge over them. It was a double jeopardy for me! I would not win on any level with the lower-level staff. I had no authority over them except professionally, but they were out of my control. On one hand, they saw me as one of those foreigners who came to America to take away their jobs. On the other side, they did not have the qualifications needed to do the RN job. Some of the bolder ones would shout at me, "Go back to your country." Some called me N-word names. N person calling N-names, how ridiculous was that ha ha!

The staff that gave me the "hardest way to go" were the low-level black Americans. One would think that I would be more welcome by my fellow black people but no. Someone once told me that some black people felt antagonistic to foreign blacks due to this sentiment, that the ancestors of foreign black people were the ones who sold black American ancestors into slavery in America. I was also told that a lot of black Americans yearn to know their African roots and have not been able to figure it out. That had nothing to do with me! But here I am many years later suffering for the "sins" of my ancestor.

As written in the bible: "The Lord, the Lord God.......by no means clearing the guilty, visiting the iniquity of the fathers upon the children and the children's children to the third and the fourth generation." Exodus 34:6 -7 (KJV). If it was really true that the iniquities of the father visit the children and grandchildren, I pray that, that iniquity will never visit my children or my grandchildren. It must end with me, the third and fourth generation of the guilty ones have already been satisfied in my generation!!

Being very new in America, I did not know how to deal with their resentment and antagonism. I had not been acclimated to the culture well enough to be able to fight back. I had a difficult time adjusting to my new life in America due to working in what appeared to be a toxic environment. What was my recourse? I had no power over any of them nor able to discipline anyone. Reporting them to the supervisor brought more of their wrath. Sometimes, I got taunted as being "a cry baby" for reporting them to the supervisor (mama) the next morning. The treatment I received from some of my fellow black people in America was difficult to fathom.

Why would I receive such treatments? I considered going back to Nigeria at many points because I felt I would not put up with that nonsense from low level staff, considering the respect I got from such level of staff when I was in Nigeria. I would come home from work and felt so dejected. I asked my husband to let me go home but he encouraged me to endure. He said coming to America was a lifetime opportunity. I needed to make the most of it since I am already there. But it was not my desire to come to America to stay in the first place. I thought to myself, *If I made and saved enough money for my air ticket, I would jump in the next plane and get out of here.*" So, it was the way I planned it. Did I stick to that plan??

I needed to also buy those clothes, shoes, handbags and some other nice things before going home. Therefore, I must work. To work, I must figure out a way to get along with the staff to make life easy for myself. I thought about what I could do to buy them over. One would think that my fellow black people would be more friendly. Some of the white staff were just indifferent but not nasty. Some were approachable and offered little help but with limit. I was not a new nurse when I came to America. But being new in America, I needed more time to learn the way things were done. Not providing adequate orientation at the beginning was very disadvantageous to me. It took me longer to catch up because I was practically teaching myself everything by reading nursing books.

Some of the areas I had problem with was misunderstanding some of the American semantics. Say for example, instead of saying "If I were you, I would do … this way…", Americans said "I would do it this way…….". Which I understood as they would do…. not knowing they were saying I should be doing it…. I got into trouble once in a situation of patient care. The patient was ordered to have a nursing procedure which I was not very familiar with. The nurse was discussing how it was done when she was handing over to me. Instead of saying "you should do it like this…" she said "I will do it like this…" which I thought in the actual sense, she was telling me how she should be doing it. Consequently, the patient ended up not getting the procedure that was ordered for him because I thought the other nurse said she was going to do it. One other example was double negative question like "Is the door not locked?" which the answer "yes" means the door is locked, while I understood the question to mean "yes" it is not locked.

Working in the rehab center was tough for me. I thought about what I could do to get my foes on my side. Knowing that I must stick around until I achieve my goal… making money enough to buy the things I wanted and get my plane ticket, I had to work and make the money. I read books on conflict resolution but found no help that could be applied to the situation I was facing. I spoke to the supervisor who did not have any reasonable answer. I considered quitting and going to another facility but I thought I would still meet the same kind of staff and start all over again. The rehab center was the second place I was treated with prejudice and disrespect. It was likely I might encounter the same treatment no matter where I went. I invoked my can-do, never-say-never attitude that I inherited from being born in Nigeria…figure out a way to make life easy for myself. An idea came to mind one day. *"Maybe if I cooked a delicious jollof rice and took it to work, I could buy them over,"* I said to myself. The worst that would happen would be they would reject the food. It worked like magic. I took a pan of jollof rice (JR) one night to work. I waited until people got hungry. I invited everyone on duty who wanted to participate to help themselves.

At first, some of the staff showed no interest. "Ain't gonna eat that African food," said some of the ladies. Even when they were very hungry, they pretended they would not eat until one of the younger ladies tasted the rice. She told the others how good it was. When they perceived the aroma of the jollof rice, they let go of their resistance and pride. All the staff on duty that night joined in the eating of "that African food" they said they ain't gonna eat! It was a slam dunk! They all had a "ball" with my rice and almost fought over the leftover to go home with. What a pan of jollof rice could do! I gained an instant fame…the jollof rice did it. I won! I won! No more trouble from my adversaries…. right?

The story of my jollof rice circulated around the center. Everyone loved it. Those who were not on duty that night regretted not being there, after they heard so much of how good the rice was. I began to get requests for jollof rice which I gladly provided. To maintain the relationship, I took Jollof rice to work every now and then. Some people who never spoke to me most of the time I had been there, asked me to make jollof rice for their family dinners and private parties at home. I had no problem doing it for them. Even the supervisor heard staff raving about the jollof rice and asked me for a sample. She too liked it. Thanks to the enormous power of jollof rice. My tenure at the rehab center became a fairly good experience from then on. For any immigrant who would experience the kind of treatment meted to me in my early years in America, I suggest trying jollof rice!

There were some prejudices I encountered which jollof rice could not solve, the outright discrimination and bigotry rampant in the mainstream America. I had been working at the rehab center close to three years and was never promoted. My salary remained twelve dollars per hour. There came a new nurse out of nursing school who was being paid fifteen dollars an hour. She was white. I was training that nurse whose salary was higher than mine. I knew what her salary was because I heard her discussing it with another nurse on the unit. I approached the supervisor to discuss my concern. My supervisor told me she was looking into it. She was looking into it for the next three months. When I realized she was not doing anything about it, I did not understand why I was being treated that way. I have been a good and hardworking nurse. There was no reason for her not to bring my salary at least up to the level of the new nurse other than prejudice.

I did not know then other recourses available to me to get what I rightly deserved. I did not know I could grieve it. With my God given attitude, I did not let my spirit be defeated by all the prejudices. I was raised to believe we do not wait for opportunities come knocking on our door, we chase it. I started looking for another job. Luckily, within one month, I found another at the Liberty medical center in west Baltimore. I went for the interview and in about three weeks, they called me. My salary was twenty dollars an hour. My supervisor promptly received my resignation letter and off to Liberty I went.... that was in 1985.

Liberty medical center was a one hundred and forty bed community hospital situated at 2600 Liberty Heights Avenue, across from Mondawmin Mall. It had four levels of inpatient beds, laboratory, physical therapy, pharmacy and clinics. There were operating and recovery rooms. I was employed initially on seven east unit which was predominantly medical and surgical patients. Some of the patients were elderly with many chronic problems. Some were nursing home patients that were incontinent and required total care. My experience at the rehab center was beneficial because by then I had mastered the art of hands-on patient care. I still abhorred cleaning "behinds" but endured it.

The staff at the Liberty medical center comprised of what I called the "United Nations". Some of the nurses were from other parts of Africa like Sierra Leone, and Liberia. They were black like me. Some were from Europe - whites, others from Haiti - blacks, and some from Philippines... brown. Then there were the Americans; a mix of black and white, and me a Nigerian... black. In the 1980's there were very few Nigerians in Baltimore so there was none in any of my workplaces. I was the only Nigerian in seven east unit at the time. On staff meetings, there were discussions about teamwork and cooperation among all staff. But that was easier said than done. I would come to learn that the United Nations were not so united after all, each nation huddled into their little groups after morning meetings.

After the assignments were done, everybody joined their subgroup or "click" and did their work cooperatively. After my orientation, I found myself slowly being alienated from the groups. I was always on my own doing my assignment. I tried extremely hard to join a "click" as there were many of them, the Americans, the Indians, the Africans, the Filipinas and the whites. None of the clicks accepted me. Even the African click was difficult to "penetrate". Every time I tried to be friendly by being nice and helpful to them, there was no reciprocation. When I needed help and called any of them, I got excuses. I was always the last to go home every day from work. I reported their treatment to the manager, I got taunted again by the groups as a "cry baby". Instead, I was making more enemies for myself.

From that time, I made up my mind I had to survive this America, one way or another. No more reporting to anyone. No more making my situation worse by reporting them to the manager. I resigned myself to being the last to going home every day and took time to do my work. So far, Liberty medical center was the third place I experienced this kind of treatment. Not only did my fellow staff show prejudice against me, but some of the patients did too.

A lot of times, some white patients were prejudiced against black nurses which I call "nurse abuse". Those patients were in their 80's and 90's. I never knew that patients in American hospitals could be very nasty to nurses who were working to save their lives. In Nigeria, nurses commanded great respect from everyone, especially from patients ill in the hospital and their families. I had so many encounters with such patients in my career in the USA. I will only mention here a few of them, most notably was my interaction with a Mr. Carter (name changed to protect the patient's privacy) at the liberty medical center, my first experience with patient abuse of a nurse.

Mr. Carter was 95 years old World War II veteran admitted to the hospital for a urinary tract infection. He was reported to be angry and nasty to the nurses. I had been off from work for a couple of days during the time of his admission, so I had no idea that none of the nurses wanted to take care of him because he was verbally and sometimes physically abusive. He was assigned to me that day. As was my normal routine, I made rounds on all my patients to introduce myself as their nurse for the day. When I got to Mr. Carter, and introduced myself, he shouted at me, "Where the hell are you from?" I tried to keep cool and answered him in toned down voice. "I am from Nigeria," I answered. He yelled again, "They brought all these niggers here who can't speak English. I don't want to see you near me. I don't want any nigger to be my nurse today. Get the hell out of here." I left the room and reported to the manager about my encounter with him. In the end, he was assigned to a white nurse.

Mr. Carter was not the only patient I endured abuse from. There was a patient who threw his cup of coffee at me in protest for me (the nigger) bringing his medicine to him. It was very humiliating when one got attacked by someone he/she was caring for. The patient was a fifty-five-year-old man. "The patient is always right" was a concept the nurse was trained to remember in all encounters with patients. Now tell me, have I done anything to deserve the patient abusing me in that manner? Does serving the patient his morning medication a reason to be abusive to me his nurse? There were so many other stories of my encounter with patients who abused me because I was black and immigrant. They called me names, they cursed at me, they threw food/drinks at me, they shouted at me to go back to where I came from, or they rejected me as care provider to them. I needed a friend, a confidant or someone to unload on or vent to, someone who could offer me an idea how to deal with the situation I found myself in the workplace. There was no one at the time. I had not met many Nigerian's who have been in America longer than I was.

At some point, it happened so frequently and getting on my nerves so badly. I began to consider fighting back the physical abuses by patients, especially the throwing of objects at me. The next time a patient threw his drink at me, I told my nurse manager that I would press charges against the patient for assault. I was told, "You will not press charges against a patient in the hospital bed. It will become a big news media circus and the authorities will not have that in this hospital. You may lose your job here if you do, and you may not find another job anywhere else as an RN because of the stigma on you." Really? The stigma follows me wherever I go in America.

My conclusion was that prejudice against immigrants of color must be the immigrants' induction into the American society, "the rite of passage". Am I right? I took it then that I must go through these abuses and prejudices in order to qualify to be a member of the American society. I had to make up my mind to survive in America or pack up and leave without getting the things I wanted. A lot of times I said to myself, *"Rita, you have to endure and get what you are here for. Remember how far you have come. Be patient, it will be well."* My personal admonition was only short-lived, it helped me get through that day. I would face the same troubles the next workday.

Knowing what I came to know years later, my supervisor had lied to me. She deceived me into believing that I would lose my job if I pressed charges against an abusive patient. The scariest thing she said was that I would not be able to find another job elsewhere if I filled a lawsuit against a patient in the hospital. I had no recourse to ward off such abuses. I did not want to put myself in a position where a "stamp of stigma" would follow me around. Not being able to find another job would become existential for me, which would mean I would leave America prematurely. After careful consideration of my options, I just had to grin and bear it, believing that was my fate as an American immigrant. I would then hang on hope that things would get better in the future.

Chapter 4

Changing Immigration Status

While working at the rehabilitation center, I found out I was pregnant with my first child. Even when I had accumulated enough money for my air ticket, I was not in a position to travel. It was a bittersweet moment for me. On one hand, I was happy to be expecting. On the other hand, my plan to go back to Nigeria was uncertain. Should I go back to Nigeria with pregnancy? My husband and I did not think it was a good idea. Going back to Nigeria plan then got shelved. It became apparent that I would need to stick around longer than I would wish. So, in the fall of 1981, I decided to enroll at the University of Maryland Baltimore County, to get my Bachelor's degree in Nursing, while waiting for the arrival of our baby. That meant I had to change my immigration status from F2 (spouse of immigrant student) to F1 (full time student). F1 student is required to carry a minimum of twelve credits every semester. I put another requirement on myself, which was to hurry my education up and head home. For that reason, I took fifteen credits per semester which I believed would cut down my time in school.

It was a difficult time: working, pregnant and going to school. My "plate" was too full to handle. Balancing schoolwork, assignments, quizzes and writing papers with working night shift, going to antenatal clinics, and meeting family life obligations became too exhausting and exasperating. The hours in the day were never long enough for all the activities of my day. The main motivator to hurry it up was returning to Nigeria as soon as possible. My husband was also in school, working to finish his doctorate degree. As I was progressing along in the pregnancy, I had to stop working and focused more on the schoolwork. Our finances suffered a major decline. We barely had enough to pay the rent and put food on the table, but we managed. I went along well in my pregnancy.

My first motherhood

On October 15th, 1981, our first son was born at the then City Hospital in Eastern Avenue in Baltimore, currently Johns Hopkins Bayview Medical Center. My first experience of motherhood was an incredibly happy time. I looked at the baby's beautiful face and thanked God for him. We named him Henry, the name Peter chose. I chose his Igbo name; Abiaziem translated, my journey was blessed. My joy was clouded in apprehension. How would I be able to take care of this "bundle of joy" with all that I had to do? As a nurse, I knew how to take care of my baby. But sleepless nights, diaper changing, frequent feeding, doctor visits and which products in the market could I afford to give the baby the best care were my challenges. Our joy was dampened by having no help. My husband was mine and the baby's caregiver, a skill he had to learn in a hurry.

In the Nigerian culture, a new mother would be pampered by family. That was a time of joy in the family, both core and extended. The new mother's mother or mother in-law would come to stay for weeks to do "omugwo" (taking care of the new mother and the baby). The new mother did nothing for the first two months except to feed the baby. Once the baby was fed, the new mother would hand over the baby to her mother or whoever else came for omugwo. They took care of the baby in the night giving the new mother time to get a restful night sleep. The new mother would eat meals made with special herbs, spices and plenty of meat and fish. What I missed the most was the new mother's special food.

None of the special herbs and spices for cooking new mother's food was available in America. Besides, I did not think of bringing those spices with me on coming to America, because I did not think I would be having babies so soon after coming. However, my husband was preparing my meals but would not know how to make the new mother's food even if we had the ingredients. I cried for my mother the first couple of weeks after birth, there was nothing I could do about my situation. We had not developed a network of friends that could be useful at the time. I realized crying was not going to help in any way. I wiped my tears, decided I was going to do the best I could…my can-do attitude, then moved on.

The Tragedy

The story of my life in America will not be complete without discussing the tragedy that befell us the second year. Henry was tragically killed in an auto accident. The story of Henry was one that has been buried beneath the depth of my heart. Even now after so many years had passed, thinking of him brought the episode fresh in my mind. All the pain and agony would surface again though to a lesser intensity. Henry's birthday, October 15th, 1981 was exactly ten months after I arrived in America. An extremely healthy and vibrant child, he was never sick, not one day! He grew up fast as if he knew his parents were suffering. He walked at the age of seven and half months. Two months before Robert was born, my husband and I were driving to Glen Burnie Maryland, to see a different doctor (obstetrician). I was seven months pregnant with Robert and did not like my obstetrician then. A friend recommended the doctor in Glen Burnie, so I got appointment to see him. Close to Glen Burnie exit on US route 295 south, we were rear ended, and Henry sustained massive head injury with him on a child safety car seat.

    I was knocked out unconscious for what seemed like eternity but was only a few minutes. I woke up to see ambulance crew working on my child. He was airlifted to Johns Hopkins Children's Trauma Center and put on life support. He died in eight agonizing days later. He was exactly one year old. It was the worst day of my life. It was the most painful experience of my life. No one would wish that kind of pain on one's worst enemy. It felt like the world had ended for me. With no friends and limited contact with relatives, the grief overwhelmed me.

    It was in the days when technology was not the way they are now. Sending and receiving messages were by letters, telegrams or telephone for those who had them in their homes. Those without phones would pay money to NITEL, a (Public telephone company in Nigeria), to make their calls. None of our family members had phones in the homes. They would call us when they went to the Nitel, but we had no way of reaching them unless they called. We could write letters, but letters took up to two months to reach their destinations. It took several weeks for messages to reach our people to inform them that we lost Henry. By that time, we had already begun to pick up the pieces and moving on.

It took a lot of time before I was able to pick myself up emotionally. The trauma of losing Henry has lasted me a lifetime. For years, I blamed myself for the accident, I was the one driving. I also asked God why He let my child be killed in the accident. I blamed God for disappointing me. Even after Robert was born, I still could not shake off the guilt feeling. I dove deep into depression. However, the birth of Robert around Christmas provided a little diversion from my feelings. Robert became my Christmas and consolation gifts in 1982. But I had this weird fear that I had been disappointed by God once. He might disappoint me again! I found it hard to sleep in the night because I was afraid something would go wrong. I would be up watching my baby sleep and so missed my own sleep time. It was very exhausting. I focused all my attention on taking care of Robert which ameliorated the grief I was feeling to some level where I could function, but still felt depressed.

That depressive feeling continued for the next three years. The symptoms were causing me health problems requiring numerous doctor visits and diagnostic testing which yielded no treatable results. My doctor suggested I went into counselling which I did. Six months into counselling, saw no discernable benefits. The doctor next suggested antidepressants. They worked as long as I took them. But I was not taking antidepressants the rest of my life! I decided to kick the pills, and trusted my faith and my inner power to overcome the depression. With prayers and soliloquys admonishing myself, those feelings slowly faded away around the time my youngest child Victor was born…. three years later. The memory of Henry lives on, deep down in my heart and this book is dedicated to his very short life.

It is worth noting here that our bereavement exposed us to the many good and generous people of America. Though only a fraction of American people were the hard-core racists and bigots, their actions made huge lasting impression on me and at the time, it felt like all Americans were racists. When we lost Henry, we received help from St. Ignatius Catholic church. The priest, Father Robert Pasquet arranged all the funeral and covered the burial expenses. Never asked us to pay a penny of it. Derby Martin, my supervisor at the rehab center was exceptionally helpful to me. She paid us visits frequently, brought us food and gave us encouragement. I am forever grateful to them.

Picking Up The Pieces

I went back to school in the spring of 1983 at the time I was still reeling from my devastating tragedy. I needed time to grieve but did not have such time. My demeanor could be compared to one in a "fog", or a blur. To be honest, I have no memory of how that semester went. I was functioning like a zombie! At the end of the semester, my courses were cleared. How I did it, I could not tell. Undergraduate studies were easier because the required subjects were duplication of the nursing courses I covered in Nigeria. It took three semesters to clench my Bachelor's degree in Nursing.

I graduated in December 1984, the year our third son, Paschal was born. As already mentioned, to maintain the F1 status, an immigrant must be enrolled in school every semester and carry a minimum of twelve undergraduate credits or nine graduate credits. Otherwise, the immigrant would violate immigration mandates and face deportation. I was not ready to go back to Nigeria at the time. With two children all under three years old, my husband and I decided we needed more resources to establish ourselves in Nigeria if we decided to go. We decided to stick around a little while longer to finish school. In order not to violate my immigrant status by staying, I enrolled in the graduate program in the fall of 1985.

Working, going to graduate school and taking care of our two children got increasingly difficult. At that time, I found out I was pregnant with Victor. The need for child-care help became even more critical. My husband and I discussed bringing help from Nigeria. My mother at the time was the best candidate to invite. Mother declined coming because her commitments would not allow her to come at the time. Sad to say, mother repeatedly declined coming to America until she passed away in 1993 after she battled cancer for about six months. I later found out her reason was fear of flying. It was so disturbing to hear that the main reason mother declined coming to America was her fear of flying. If I had known that fact, we could have managed to bring her to America. She would have been sedated to fly. Maybe she could have received treatment in America for the cancer that killed her so early in life. Maybe she could have survived the cancer. She died in December 1993 at the age of 59. Mother, may you rest in perfect peace.

Where does help come from?

The only option for child-care left to consider was daycare, which I did not like, due to horror stories I heard about some daycare mothers who abused children. A friend once told me that her daycare mother drugged her child. Her daughter was limp when she went to pick her up one day. My friend rushed the baby to the hospital where it was discovered that the woman had given the baby phenobarbital (a heavy sedative). It was a common practice among daycare mothers, to keep the children sleeping so they would not be bothered. The child would have died if my friend was not quick to rush the baby to the hospital where she was given an antidote. So many stories which were very concerning!

I also heard that some daycare mothers were beating the children, sometimes using curse words before the children. Some people said some of the care mothers engaged in intimacy with their significant others in front of the little ones! It is a well-known fact that children emulate what they see or hear. I did not want to expose my children to such a potentially immoral or deadly treatment. We decided the children would remain at home until they were old enough to attend grade school. Being a nurse gave me the flexibility to work around the children's routines. I took night shift jobs, watched the children in the daytime, while my husband worked daytime and watched them in the night when I was at work. It was not an easy feat raising children without childcare help. As stated, I was working on my Master's degree, and working at the rehab center as well.

Victor was born a few days before the spring semester in 1986. Can anyone imagine leaving a two-week old infant at home to go to school or work? That was the fate and the destiny of an immigrant like me in those years. My heart almost broke for leaving my infant and two toddlers at home, missing all the infant-mother bonding time. Even when I wanted to breast-feed my babies, I was not able to manage it for a long time like the working mothers of today. My baby had infant allergies to baby formula. That posed more challenges to my problem. It took time to find an appropriate formula for him.

I always told the young couple of today who have their parents come to America to help them with child-care, they should thank their God. They do not know how good they have it. They are able to leave the house and run some errands knowing that their children are being taken care of. They are confident their children are not being abused by crazy care mothers. They can go out on date nights with their spouses or go to parties on the weekend. In my own case, even for small errands, I always went along with the children. It took longer to pack up the children going and coming. The children could never be left alone for a short time, even if it were for a few minutes. It was very exhausting.

A friend told me a story of how she landed in jail for leaving her children alone for a short time. My friend had three children, the oldest was five and the youngest was two years old. She needed to run out to the store to get a few items. She dreaded having to pack up the children with her, so she decided to go when they took their afternoon nap. She came home to find the two-year-old missing. Apparently, the baby somehow left the house. He was walking along the road in diapers only, looking for his mother. Someone saw the baby and called police. My friend was charged with child abuse and neglect which bought her a short jail time. When I thought about my friend's story, the children were always with me no matter how short the errand was. Growing up, my children were almost same in size. Sometimes Robert and Paschal would be mistaken for twin. Later Victor caught up with them in growth and all three of them would be mistaken for triplets.

Lothian road

We lived in the second-floor apartment on Lothian Road when Victor was born. We had just moved to that apartment from downtown Baltimore two months before. A middle-aged Indian doctor and his wife were living on the first floor below us. The neighbor on the first floor had problem with the thumping of the feet of two toddlers on the second floor. When we first moved in, the doctor was friendly, greeted us well and told us his occupation. Within the first week, he came up almost every day to complain about the children making noise. He told my husband to figure out a way to stop the children from walking on a carpeted floor! He became a nuisance because he would come up and banged on our door multiple times during the day. Sometimes he would bang on his ceiling, which was our floor when he felt my children were disturbing him. At some point, we had to ignore him. He reported us to the apartment management and threatened them he would move if they did not make us leave.

The management company sent multiple warnings to us to control our children. We would not tie the children in one place so they will not run or jump in the house like children do. After multiple appeals, both the management and the neighbors were unreasonable. We were told we needed to move because the doctor was threatening to leave if we did not. The manager said that tenant was a long-tenured tenant they did not want to lose, so we must be the ones to move. The controversy continued for the next month.

When he came up the next time to accost us about children making noise, my husband was so enraged. My husband met the neighbor at the door with a hammer and threatened to break his head. I was so afraid and thought the worst could happen. He could land in jail for either assault or murder depending on what ended up happening. I would then be left with the children alone and he would rack up criminal history. I was not going to let that happen. We made a hasty decision to move into a townhouse on McCabe Avenue, about two miles down the road from Lothian road.

We did not know the area very well. We came to learn McCabe street was a drug infested neighborhood. It appeared there was a drug dealer market in front and behind the house we lived in. Every night we heard voices and footsteps around the house. I was scared to death. We thought about moving again. But we had just moved into that house, not moving again so soon! The incident that happened about two weeks after we moved into the house was "the straw that broke the camel's back"!

One night around 1 am, I was woken by helicopter noise that landed in front of the house we lived in. There was a gun battle in the house opposite us. I looked out of the window to see what was going on. Air ambulance had just arrived to carry the victims of the shootings. Multiple murders had occurred! I saw victims being loaded in the ambulance. When that murder occurred at the building across from us, we made the decision to move out of there immediately, but we did not want to move into a place where we would have to move again soon.

So, renting a house made more sense. We wanted a whole house where we would not go through what we have been through in Lothian road. We have to rent the house in a good neighborhood. Were we ready to be homeowners in America? No, we were not ready. We began the search for a house to rent.

Buying the home on Sagra Road

On Beninghouse road, I saw a "to rent" sign in front of a house. I called the number on the sign and a real estate agent named Claude Edline answered. I could detect from his accent that he was from the Islands. Claude was from Haiti. When I told him my intention to rent the house at Beninghouse, Claude said, "I can help you buy a house instead of renting."

"I am only interested in renting," I said.

He said, "Why don't we meet and talk about it in my office?" So, he scheduled an appointment for me and my husband to meet with him in his office in Towson Maryland.

Being an immigrant too, I trusted every word Claude said. I was so much interested in knowing how he was so successful in America. Claude told us his immigrant stories and his adversities in America too. He discussed his own American journey and the prejudices he endured. He told us how he got to where he was then, how he had acquired real estates which have become solid investments for him and his family. He owned apartment buildings which yielded money for him. He traveled to Haiti very often to see his family there and said, "Someday you could do that too". He would soon retire to the Islands and let his children manage his real estates. I was not interested in the later statement because I had made up my mind to go back to Nigeria.

In my mind, I was suffering too much and would prefer to be in a place where I would have reliable help to raise our children. We told him of our plan to leave USA once we completed our education.

In the end, Claude managed to convince us that buying a house is better than renting.

"A house will grow in equity and also provides tax shelter during tax season." His statements were way over my head then. That was my first time hearing the word "equity" in relation to houses and tax shelter. "But if you rent", he continued, "the tax exemption benefits the landlord." He asked me a few questions about my job and how much I was making on weekly bases. "You can buy a house you know with the money you both make".

The decision to buy the house was difficult because we still had our minds on moving back to Nigeria. The suffering without childcare was great. I always thought we would be better off if we moved back to Nigeria. There, we would have plenty of help in raising the children and making life easier on ourselves. The conclusion in the end was that we would take Claude at his words and buy the house. But the house would be sold when we get ready to leave United States. So, we bought our first house in America... 5618 Sagra Road in Baltimore with the help of Claude Edline. It was a three-bedroom town house. At the time, it was perfect for our young family. My husband and I with two toddlers and the baby. I am always grateful to Claude for the help!

My personality is one that likes to have a clean and well-organized house. With the children, the house was always disorganized most of the time. I felt like screaming; clothes, toys, pots and dishes littered all over the floor. My children like making music with the pots, pans and the spoons. All the kitchen cabinets were always wide open with their contents on the floor. After picking them up, they found their way back on the floor. Three active boys close in age, tearing the house up! It was an exceedingly difficult time for me.

Once after working a terribly busy night shift, I came home very tired. My husband had made breakfast for us and got the children ready for school. Even when I was too sleepy, I still had to drop the children off to school, which was what I did Monday to Friday during school season. Baby was with me. Immediately I got back home from dropping Robert and Paschal off to school, I quickly ate my breakfast and slumped into the sofa and fell asleep with the dishes and cutlery still on the coffee table. The baby climbed into the sofa with me and tried to wake me up. The next thing I knew, the baby was using the fork to pry my left eye open. "Mommy, wake up," he said. I sure did wake up alright, and ended up in the emergency room with a left eye injury.

When can we go back to Nigeria? We did not have a social life. We had no respite from the children. I thought I was losing my mind. Some days I wondered when we would have a normal life. I also thought about the amount of help I would have had if I had been in Nigeria. I would have had at least two maids if not more. I have people who would be incredibly happy to live with us and help me with the children. Here I am all alone with my husband raising three children with our other commitments. I was always exasperated. I cried sometimes when I thought about how much better life would be for us if we had child-care help. The thought of moving back to Nigeria intensified in my mind. I have got to finish my Master's degree and leave United States was always on my mind!

Our situation was compounded by demands from home. In Nigeria, it was believed that those outside Nigeria were better off than them especially those in America. The expectation from family there was high. It did not matter that the person was still a student, or have family responsibilities. It was believed that the person who lived in America would be able to offer help to family members at home. We were getting requests for our family's children's school fees, money for sick family members to go to hospital, some wanted money to start business, some needed money to buy cars for car business, some want help to bring them to America, Etcetera; the stories were endless.

If they truly knew what we were going through, some of them would not want to come to America. As was customary, we would send money home to take care of the family members who needed help, but not for buying cars. As a result, we were never able to save money enough to take our leave of the USA as we planned.

For us to be ready to leave USA, we needed to have basic things to start life in Nigeria. Those were a house, we purchased a three-bedroom bungalow in Owerri, Imo state a couple of years before.

We needed a car, prospects of getting jobs in the city and good schools for our children. At that time, the Marist Brother's primary and secondary schools in Uturu, Okigwe was reported to be the best school in the then Imo state for the children. That gave us hope that the children would get good education. The prospects of finding good jobs especially for my husband was not guaranteed. It would be easier for me to get a job in any hospital, me being in health care field. What about mobility? Should we buy a car and ship to Nigeria?

As the years went by, it became more and more complicated and financially involving in planning and executing our return to Nigeria. We were not able to pull it off after making multiple attempts. It became likely that we would stay longer in America, at least for the meantime, to work and save money. With the family growing, our needs were multiplying. The children were all about to start grade school and got involved in multiple extracurricular activities. We were drawn to so many different directions trying to meet up with the children's activities and our own needs. No matter how much money we made, we rarely had money left over at the end of the month. Before I knew it, life had become more and more hectic.

Chapter 5

The Settlement

Time went amazingly fast. The children were growing like weeds. Within a short time, our oldest child Robert had gotten old enough to attend grade school. What should we do now? At first, we discussed packing up everybody and heading home in the late 80's. We did not want the children to grow up in America. Our reason was based on stories we heard about children succumbing to peer pressures, using drugs and joining gangs especially male children. The stories were endless about young boys going astray, getting killed on the streets of Baltimore. We had all male children, and the news was genuinely concerning. But we were not financially ready to leave for good. Besides, the news from Nigeria was: "The economy is bad. Not a good time to come home." With private schools promising better education, there was consideration that the children would go to school in one of them had we decided to go. But with those reports about Nigeria, we were hesitant to go. Besides, I considered leaving my children in the hands of other people no matter how trustworthy they were, was equivalent to having somebody else raise my children. No! I would not do that.

Other parents of the Nigerian origin were nursing the same sentiments like us. Parents who could afford private schools in Nigeria and had people they trusted to care for their children did so. We considered sending our children there but did not have trusted support there. Stories emerged that some parents who had sent their children there for schooling were regretful of the idea because the support for the children was not what was promised. The money those parents were sending to relatives to care for the children was embezzled. The school fees got paid but the children's care was neglected. Some of those children went astray instead.

But wait! Does it make sense that the same schools we abandoned years before, due to what we considered as poor-quality education, would be a place where we were considering sending our children? After careful consideration, we cancelled the idea. We decided it would be best if we all go together rather than sending them alone. We planned to stick around a little to raise money. We thought it wise to take them to Nigeria every summer, try hard to inculcate our heritage, culture, language and morals in them while we wait for the best time to leave US.... hoping it would not be too long. At the time we were done with school, my husband has gotten his doctoral degree, and I got my master's degree. Not financially ready, we needed to stick around to work and save money for our final exit. Our immigration status needed to change to resident alien (green card) for us to be able to work. We applied for green card.

In 1988, we were invited to receive our green card at the American Embassy in Nigeria. We took the opportunity to visit family while we were there. We came back to Baltimore, with a goal of returning to Nigeria finally in three or four years, which did not happen. The plan to take the children to Nigeria every summer became a tall order due to financial constraints. A family of five to travel to Nigeria involved multiple thousands of dollars. We thought it wise to build our home in our village first so that we would have a comfortable place to stay while we worked to establish ourselves.

So, we embarked on building our house in the village. In those days, people did not depend on mortgages to finance their homes. Homes were built with money in hand or borrowed from family and friends. A lot of money went into building houses, so people built them in stages according to the amount of money they had. It took us four years to complete the house. It was a beautiful eight-bedroom house in the heart of the village. I dreamt of the time our family would move back to occupy that beautiful home we built. But, unfortunately, my wish would only get stuck in my dream. My wish is yet to come true, but when? The house in the village is currently occupied by family members.

Alas! The children were growing up fast in America. Going back to Nigeria was not an option. We had no other choice but to settle down in America! There was apprehension that being born in America, children may lose their ethnic identity and culture. Our belief was that our legacy were our children. How we raise them determines the quality of humanity we will leave for the world. No number of our other achievements will compensate for not raising our children properly. Inculcating into them our culture was of paramount importance. Our success without raising our children as decent human beings who will contribute great things to society meant we have failed in our duty as parents. What schools should the children attend? Private vs public schools?

Though public schools were and still are free for primary education, we decided on private schools for the following reasons: discipline and strong academics. Our children are all boys. As boys are more likely to get in trouble or influenced by bad company, we thought private school would teach them discipline and at the same time offer them quality academics and good role models in the teachers and coaches. Private schools had their own problems; however, I believe any parents who are able to sacrifice so much for their children's education have same value as we had. It provided me with peace of mind that the children would have good role models and friends. That decision paid off greatly as discussed in later pages of this book.

In the early 80's, people from Nigeria increased in number in Baltimore. A growing number of Igbo speaking parents were worried that their children are missing out on the rich Igbo culture and language, hence sharing in our concerns. What can be done? A group of parents got together to discuss what to do. The idea of forming an organization whose mission was primarily to promote and celebrate the Igbo culture, teach our children the culture and the language came up. It would also be a medium where people could go to reach out to other Nigerians in times of need. It would give the children a medium to meet each other and hopefully develop relationship with someone of similar ethnicity with hope they would develop a long-term relationship, which would culminate in marriage, as some parents preferred their children to marry an Igbo descent.

The Igwe Bu Ike Association, translated: (There is strength in number), was formed in the mid 80's. The Igbo speaking Nigerians met on Saturdays with their children. They discussed ways to propagate the Igbo culture in America and the children would meet in small groups where they were taught primarily Igbo language. The teachers were Igbo speaking volunteers. Cultural events were planned to showcase our rich Igbo culture and heritage, such as New Yam Festival, which was a big cultural celebration in Igbo land to mark annual harvest. The new yam festival was a celebration when farmers harvest first crop of the year and celebrate by thanking God for a rich harvest. That would be the event when people begin to eat yam for the first time during that farming season. There were fashion shows, cooking contests, singing competitions and children's programs, etc. The organization was growing and needed a place where they could have their gatherings. At that time, Igwe Bu Ike was having their gatherings in borrowed spaces like in church or community halls.

To remain strong, members of any organization must cultivate and propagate virtues of love of their fellow members, humility, and willingness to help the organization when called upon. Misunderstanding regarding where to build their cultural center escalated into open confrontations among the leadership. Disagreement about who would lead the organization also came up. Nepotism reared its ugly head as it sometimes did in Nigeria. Different factions lobbied for their friends or people from their town be elected to office. Some people wanted the center to be positioned in West Baltimore closer to them. Another group wanted it to be in the East Baltimore closer to them. Yet another wanted it in the north. Unfortunately, disagreement regarding where to build the center and nepotism killed the project. Igwe Bu Ike lasted only a few years and collapsed.

An association of that magnitude required strong leadership for it to thrive. Igwe bu Ike association did not have strong committed members who would carry on its affairs. Igwe bu Ike depended mostly on volunteers who were mostly seeking their own self-interests. "What is in this for me?" It was not long before Igwe Bu Ike disintegrated into oblivion in the late 80's. Up 'till today, I personally did not know what happened to all the money collected to build the cultural hall which was in the thousands of dollars.

It was very common in Nigeria for people who have custody of public money to commit embezzlement. That is why even today, people from Nigeria do not trust one another when it comes to public money. Embezzlement is the order of the day in Nigeria and that is one corruption that will never end in my opinion. Igbo indigens in the diaspora are capable in reviving Nigeria if they could show honesty and commitment in handling public money. But people are hesitant to contribute money to any cause in Nigeria because there is this nagging thought that the money may not be used for the intended purpose and may end up in the pockets of those trusted with it.

As more and more parents of the Igbo speaking Nigerians yearned for a medium to help their children learn the language and culture, other organizations came into being, mostly Christian/faith-based organizations. In the mid 90's, the Nigerian Igbo Catholic Community (NICC) was born. NICC was, and still is Catholic organization formed with a mission to "provide an environment for all Igbos in the Baltimore Metropolitan area to worship in their native language, Igbo, and to cultivate a lasting fraternal community among the people whereby morals and Christian values are cherished".

The organization provided and still provides spiritual guidance to Igbo children and facilitates the assimilation of newly arrived Igbos into local parishes. NICC started popping up in numerous communities in USA, thereby became known as NICC (Nigerian Igbo Catholic Community) in Diaspora. In addition to the women and men groups, there were children's and youth groups which catered more to the needs of the children. That was more important to most parents with young children. Those organizations had its struggles from their inception. However, over the years, they have grown exponentially. As far as I know, NICC has remained true to its mission 'till today, giving all the Igbo speaking Nigerians and their children in diaspora some semblance of normalcy closer to their heritage, but not necessarily exactly as it is in Nigeria today.

The late 80's ushered in school shopping for our children at the time we were living in Sagra Road. Our goal was to find a school that would not only help the children academically, but also build them up with discipline and good morals. We settled on St Mary's school in Govans based on word-of-mouth by friends' recommendations. St Mary's was a private, predominantly black school attached to the St Mary's Catholic Parish Govan. Some of my friends had their children there too. It was close to our home and convenient for drop offs and pick-ups.

In the fall of 1989, the children were enrolled, Robert first, Paschal next and Victor later. The children liked going to school and were thriving there. The biggest problem for us was coming up with the school fees for three children at once. The school was gracious enough to make the fees easy monthly payments. The children had excellent grades and the teachers liked them. They were impressed regarding how smart and well behaved they were. The children were known in the school with a nickname: "the three musketeers". None of them got in serious trouble that came to my attention as far as I remembered. I was glad the school was true to its mission of child education and development.

To ensure that the children were thought by good teachers and receiving good teaching, I opted to attend the teachers' teaching sessions. The school allowed parents to sit in teachers' teaching sessions. I took the opportunity to observe classroom dynamics. That gave me confidence regarding the quality of the teachers and what they taught the students. I partnered with the teachers in making sure my children applied themselves seriously to their education, the same way we always emphasized the value of education at home. We have always told them education is the key to success in life. I encouraged the teachers to give them additional homework to keep them engaged at home with little time to watch TV or play video games.

Though sometimes I would have to assist them in completing the work which I may not have all the time to do. The idea was great as it kept them away from the TV even if it was for ten minutes less and advanced them in their learning. I participated in parent-teacher meetings, volunteered in the lunchroom, which gave me the ability to see my children in the school ground at least once a week monitoring their progress Them knowing mom was coming to the school on whatever day helped to keep them well behaved. What kid would like the teacher report to his or her mother about bad behavior in school?

St. Mary's Church Parish was where we worshiped at the time. It was a great church community where children also thrived. Both the school and the church existed to 'develop the unique, God-given gifts of each student in a safe, nurturing and diverse environment through academics, service to others and spiritual preparation for a fulfilling life that follows the footsteps of Jesus Christ'. The children learned Catholic prayers and read the scriptures. They enjoyed going to church and received their first holy communion there. I believe the children's character must have been positively impacted by the good things they learned at St. Mary's School and Church which were the first organizations they encountered.

In addition to academics, they were enrolled in the basketball program which helped to keep them engaged after school and on the weekends when they had to play championship games. In the summer, I had enrolled Robert in another school's basketball program. It was predominantly white children playing. My son was a good player at the time. I would drop him off and come back later to pick him up. Robert at age nine or ten encountered the first unspoken prejudice against blacks on the basketball court. Every time he was playing with his OWN teammates, they would not throw the ball to him. He would run around the court, not touching the ball once. "What in the world is going on?"

My son would come back from the game very dejected. I would ask him how he did in the game?

"Mom they don't like me," he said. "They don't throw ball to me".

There were only two black boys in the team. My son goes to a different school than those boys. That other black kid went to the same school with the white kids. My son experienced the same prejudice which I experienced at work. I watched the game one evening and confirmed what my son said. I had to remove Robert from that program immediately. I resented the idea that people would treat my child that way. Such treatment may cause a child to have a low self-esteem and I was not having it. My children would not go through prejudice like I went through.

I enrolled Robert in the little league sports at Cecil Kirk Amateur Athletic Association (AAU) basketball program under Coach Melvin. Cecil Kirk team was predominantly black children playing in it. Robert soared in that program and helped the team win local championships. His team went on to win national AAU championship in the thirteen-year-olds. Paschal joined the ten-year-old team, and his team also won local and national championships. Victor was recruited by Coach O'Neil at the Chick Webb AAU team for the eight-year-olds. Victor's team won local championships as well and went on to compete at the national level. I had the opportunity to travel with Victor's team to national championships at Greensborough North Carolina and Disney land Florida. My children's self-confidence and pride were built up by their achievements in those programs.

Cecil Kirk AAU and Chick Webb AAU helped develop our children athletically and provided the springboard in which they had sprung into the athletic world. We wanted the kids to develop good work ethics as they were growing up, using and maximizing their talents in the classroom and in sports. Slowly the children excelled in sports and academics. The coaches always talked about how good they have performed in the courts. The teachers also commented about their aptitude and work ethics in the classroom. The children's performances in school made us immensely proud which convinced us the investment in the private school was all worth it.

In the mid 90's, our family began outgrowing the small three-bedroom Sagra Road townhouse. Robert was going into eighth grade, Paschal was going into sixth grade and Victor in fifth. The children have grown almost six feet each. There was a need to upgrade our dwelling because we were bumping into and knocking each other down. We needed at least a four-bedroom house and were financially able to afford it at the time. We began shopping for a house. We were unable to find a four-bedroom houses in Baltimore City we liked. We stepped out to Baltimore County. In Randallstown, we found a beautiful four-bedroom single family house with a big yard in front and bigger yard in the back. It had above the ground swimming pool which the children loved so much. Buying that house would mean we would move away from the Baltimore city. It would also mean the children would have to change school.

Changing school in the last year of middle school might not have been advantageous to Robert. But we finally decided to move anyway to 9702 Ames Court on August 10th, 1995. The children were accepted in Holy Family School in Randallstown for the fall semester. They were exhilarated about moving into the new house. Each one was pleased to have their own room. The house at Sagra Road got sold but was not because we were going back to Nigeria as we planned at the beginning.

Come fall 1995, the children started school at Holy family. They were excited about the new school and making new friends. We encouraged them to enroll in sports as before. I came to find out that the curriculum in all three of the children's classes were subjects they had already covered at St Mary's School. I was extremely disappointed because it appeared my children spent a whole school year not learning anything new. Robert who was high school bound had to do extra work outside of the school in order to prepare for SAT and get ready for high school.

Paschal and Victor had to get extra homework, I made it standard for them. That was when I realized St. Mary's School in Govan was academically more superior than Holy Family School in Randallstown. I knew my children were liked by all the teachers in St Mary's School but I did not know the magnitude of their liking them until we moved. Some of the teachers lamented about not having my children in the school the coming school year. It appears the "three musketeers were the rock that held the school". There was massive exit of students when we left St Mary's. Robert's teachers at St Mary's School were very kind to attend Robert's graduation in Holy Family School due to how they liked him. Unfortunately, St. Mary's School became one of the casualties of poor enrolment. It closed its doors a few years after we left.

Racial discrimination followed us to Ames Court in Randallstown. When we first moved into the Ames, we were happy there was a mix of multi-ethnic families, but more Caucasians. We were flanked on both sides of the house by white families. On our right was a family of four, a couple and two children a boy and a girl same age as my children. On our left was a middle-aged woman with grandchildren of my children's age. We were happy Ames Court residents had a good number of young families like ours. We were thinking our children would have playmates and a mix of other children to associate with. We decided to meet and greet our new neighbors. My husband and I went over to the neighbors on our right. They were very cold, never shook our hands, made no eye contact and never reciprocated our visit. There and then, we knew they were not happy to see us move into the neighborhood. We found out later they forbade their children from playing with my children.

Ames Court was a short cul-de-sac and ended right in front of our house. Neighborhood children played at the end of the cul-de-sac in the evenings and weekends during the spring and summer. I always looked out my window to watch all the children playing on the cul-de-sac. Some days my children joined the neighborhood children to play. I did not know the adult neighbors on our right did not like my children playing with their children. One day, I heard the mother yelling at their children to come back home. After that day, those children never came outside when my children were outside. One day, one of our sons saw those children playing in their driveway and asked them to come out in the cul-de-sac as they have always done. To my children's dismay, those children retorted, "Our mom said we can't play with you anymore."

Little by little, other white kids in the neighborhood withdrew from coming out to play in the cul-de-sac. All three of my children and other black kids were the only ones who came out frequently. Instead of playing with other children in the cul-de-sac, the white kids played in their driveways. It appeared that their parents must have told them not to come out to play in the cul-de-sac with the black kids anymore.

Within two months after we moved into that neighborhood, the neighbors on the right sold their house and moved. Once the family on our right moved, there was almost like an "exodus" of most of the white families on that street. Why were they moving.... racial prejudice? They did not want black family like ours in their neighborhood. In a couple of years, the whole street turned into a predominantly black neighborhood.

Chapter 6

The bargaining chip for good grades

People always asked my husband and me if we played sports when we were younger. No, I never played any organized sports in my life. Nor did my husband. But how was it that our children were so successful in sports? It all came down to God's providence. In Nigeria, the main sports I knew that were played were basketball and soccer which neither of us played. It was indeed the training our children received in Chick Webb and Cecil Kirk that helped develop them into star athletes they later became. They won multiple awards and trophies which decorated my fireplace at our home in Ames Court.

Robert completed middle school in spring of 1995. We had his graduation party in the house. One very notable guest that attended Robert's middle school graduation party was my cousin's husband who just emigrated from Nigeria a couple of days before the party. His name was Dr. Smithson Ahiabuike. Dr. Ahiabuke was and still is a medical doctor who practiced in Nigeria for many years before coming to America. He is currently the medical director of Hope Medical Center in Gadsden Alabama. He is also a poet. When Dr. Smithson entered our house and saw all of my children's trophies and accolades laid out for all to see, he was mesmerized. He asked for a piece of paper which I immediately handed to him. He wrote a poem there and then about the success of my children. He branded my children:

MY AMERICAN ADVENTURE (2024)

"The Three Basketeers" and the poem went like this:

> Three Basketeers: Celebration of Medals
> Great and momentous occasion of honour
> When three young men of valour
> Do us proud in doing so much
> Here on a rocky pedestal lie in awe
> The power of their biceps, The youth in their shoulders
> The wisdom in their brains
>
> Doing the family proud, Doing relations proud
> Keeping the Nigerian flag in America
> They stare on the faces in their glory
> Some gold, Some silver, Some bronze, And some platinum
> Then the plaques, Then the certificates
> Adoring president Bill Clinton Autograph
> Then here and there Are the medals
> Medals here, medals there, Medals everywhere
> Even the trophies in their glamour
> Stare at us in their beauty, on their shining stands
> Young men the "three basketeers"
> The future of tomorrow we salute you in admiration
> Of what tomorrow holds, What does tomorrow hold?
> With the seer's eye
> I can see greatness, fame, valour, wealth
> And honestly in manly dignity
> Three basketeers never sleep
> Work harder and make us proud, Fulfilling your destiny
> Bravo!!

Signed: by Dr. Smithson Ahiabuike

In Spring of 1996, Robert started high school at Mt. Joseph High School in Baltimore. During the first week of school, he came home with a sign-up sheet for football. He asked me to sign him up. Previously I had introduced all three of my children to soccer game (football) as it was called in Nigeria. After about two weeks of practice, they all refused to go to practice because they did not like the game. So when Robert came home from school with a signup sheet for football, I was surprised he asked to be signed up.

"I thought you hated football" I said.

Robert stated, "No mom, the coach asked me to try out, and I want to."

I said, "Oh good, I will sign you up." I signed him up not knowing that I was signing him up for the American football! That American football I condemned when I first came to America! Is that what I signed my child up to play? At that time, I dropped and picked up Robert from school every day.

Every evening that they had football practice, it happened that I never got there on time to pick him up. So, I never saw them actually practicing. One day, I got there on time, and he was still in practice, so I waited and watched. I did not see the ball or anyone kicking the ball with foot. I was baffled! *What kind of football are they playing?* I waited 'till they were done.

When I asked Robert what game they were paying? "Football of course."

"I did not see anybody kick any ball," I declared.

"We were doing scrimmage mom," he replied.

"What is scrimmage in football?" I have never seen that before.

"We are doing a no-pad scrimmage mom." I got more and more confused.

On game day, the players were in full football gear: helmet, pad and cleats. When I arrived at the field and saw the players in full gear, I was confused again. *"What in the world is going on here? This may not be the location for the game,"* I thought. I went to the practice field, but no one was there. I came back to the football field. *"Is this the football my son made me sign him up for? Oh no, it is all a mistake."*

MY AMERICAN ADVENTURE (2024)

"My son is not going to play this game. I don't want him hurt," I thought. I signed him up for "football"- soccer. So, I cancelled Robert from the American football. I told Robert to never set foot in that field for practice or game anymore. I don't want him to have injuries, which I have seen on the TV… broken bones, head injuries and the like. Robert was very unhappy about not going to football practices. He looked incredibly sad every time I picked him up from school.

When questioned why he was sad, he said he wanted to play football. "The coach asked me today why I have not been to practice. I told him my mom said don't go."

A couple of days went by, I received a call from the coach. "This is Mike Working, the football coach at Mount St. Joe, may I speak to Mrs. Abiamiri please".

My "tentacles" went up immediately because I knew exactly why he was calling. "Yes Mr. Working, I know you are calling about Robert not coming to practice. I stopped him from going because I do not want him hurt. I don't like the game, it is too rough." Mr. Working tried to convince me, but I was persistent. In the end, he invited me for a meeting, which I reluctantly agreed to.

After school, the next day Robert and I met Mr. Working. He talked about the benefits of him playing football. "He has a potential to be an excellent player. It may even help him get college scholarship if you allow him."

"Mrs. Abiamiri if you allow me coach your son, I will make you a rich woman." I was not bought over because I was afraid of the injuries. "But injuries happen in any sports," he said.

"But not as bad as in this American football," I would say. The head injuries were very frightening. Mr. Working tried every way he could to convince me to put my son back in that rough game but was unsuccessful. No, he is not playing that game! On our way home Robert begged and begged to be allowed to go to practice and the answer was no. But when I saw how much it meant to him to play in that game, I gave him my condition for eligibility to play, which was no less than B in any class. Any semester when his grade was anything below B, he would drop out of the game. The game became the bargaining chip for good grades.

Robert took the challenge and maintained above the B average throughout high school. He played state and national championships in the All-Star games. His athleticism and scholarly achievement exposed him to become a candidate for college recruit. We had different schools calling to recruit him. Schools like US Naval Academy in Annapolis Maryland, Temple University in Philadelphia, McDaniel's College and University of Maryland were after him... to name a few. We took a trip to Annapolis to visit the US Naval Academy, but Robert was not interested. I really wanted him to go to the Naval Academy, but he did not like the military life. We gained instant fame in Baltimore because he made the news in the local newspapers and TV every weekend. He earned a scholarship to go to college and he chose the University of Maryland at College Park in the fall of 2000.

When it was Paschal's time to go into high school, he was admitted at Mount St. Joseph High School as well. Paschal wanted to play the same football which I forbade his older brother from playing two years before. He too showed earnest interest in playing, just like his brother. I gave him the same requirement of B minimum in all classes or face disenrollment from football. Paschal also turned out to be a scholar athlete as well. My boys became local celebrities, each on their own right. Weekend newspapers were plastered by pictures and stories of Abiamiri boys at Mount St. Joseph High School. Such a success makes any parent proud. We were!

On the second year of Paschal at Mount St. Joseph High School, Victor was ready to go to high school. Victor wanted to join his brothers at Mount St. Joe. But I did not want the proverbial "putting all my eggs in one basket". Coach Clachey was after him for the basketball team. Though Mount S.t Joseph High School was and still is a good school, I preferred a different school for Victor. Being a good student and an athlete, he was highly sought after by most local private schools in Baltimore area. Some of the local high schools were offering scholarship for Victor. It came down to two choices: McDonald High School in Owings Mills and Gilman School in Roland Ave.

MY AMERICAN ADVENTURE (2024)

Victor chose Gilman School and it turned out to be one of the best decisions he ever made. Victor was a star scholar athlete at Gilman School. His brothers in Mount St Joseph were also star scholar athletes. My family became local sports celebrities. Newspaper freelancers were thronging my house asking for interview which we gladly gave them. TVs and radio sports programs had segments on the Abiamiri boys on the weekends until the sports season was over.

Mount St. Joe and Gilman schools were rivals in athletics. The two schools played against each other multiple times in the school year, sometimes with my three children, two on the opposing teams of the game. Oh boy! Those games were always tough to watch. Who would I cheer for? Which jersey should I wear? To be fair to both children, I would stand at one end zone wearing Mount St. Joe Jersey and wrapping Gilman jersey around my waist. By half time, I moved over to the other end zone wearing Gilman Jersey and wrapping Mount St. Joe's jersey around my waist. On such games, I was always a spectacle in my own right. The news media and newspapers went wild with stories of me and my children! Gilman school won the game twice. We already knew Gilman was number one in the area. It was not a surprise that Gilman would win, and the contribution Victor made for their win.

I believed the game was tough for them to play too. Robert and Paschal played wide receiver on the opposing team, and Victor played defensive end at the Gilman team. I could not imagine how Victor felt knocking his older brothers down in public in the name of a game! On our way home after the game, no one was allowed to talk about the game nor at the dinner table. But, for the young Victor, he still wanted to brag…. maybe when mom and dad were not present or in close earshot. When the two schools have away games, we alternated going to one or the other because we could not be in two places at one time.

There was a day I actually had to be in two places at one time. You ask how? It was a day when Mount St. Joseph was playing their game at Calvert Hall High School, and Gilman School had their own game at Gilman with another high school. Both games happened to be starting at the same time. Which game should I attend and miss the other? They did not consider some of us who have children in different schools when they were scheduling the games. I must find a way to attend both games, so I am represented for each child. Calvert Hall High School was about fourteen minutes' drive from Gilman school. What did I do? I first went to Mount St. Joe's game at Calvert Hall and watched the game. At half time, I drove to Gilman at their half time too, and watched Gilman game when they returned for the second half of the game. I was able to attend both games played at the same time in one day. Brilliant! You say…ha ha!

Headlines like "For No. 13 Mount St. Joe vs No. 1 Gilman, Abiamiri keeping things in the family" (Sunday Sun, October 7th, 1999) were all over the news that week. We did not let the fame get into the children's heads. Our family was all about mentoring the children to aspire in achieving their highest potential in academics and anything good they do and teaching them good moral character. That became the mantra of our parenting. My children were hard working as kids in school and in sports. They were respectful to us, their parents. They carried this respectful attitude to the elders whom they met along the way.

I heard from teachers and coaches alike that they were smart, respectful and obedient children. Always did their homework. They never were in big trouble in school short of noise making in class which earned them detention after school. I would ask why they were making noise. Sometimes I did not fault them because I believed the teacher may have been unreasonable; not inquiring why the child was talking. They were never involved in any of the serious malady of drugs, alcohol or gang. I am grateful to my children for making us proud.

But our children are humans and not perfect. Though generally close to perfect, but not all the time. They went through the stages of growth and adolescence years, otherwise they would not be humans. They liked to watch TV and play video games, neglecting their chores just like any other kids. Sometimes it was repeated multiple times, sometimes with a yell before the chore got done. Keeping their rooms clean was their most difficult task. Two of them were worse in particular. I am not naming names as they would know themselves and to give them a little privacy, leaving it to the reader's imagination.

Keeping their rooms clean was the main area of conflicts in our household. They all had closets, but preferred clothes on the floor. There was no way to tell clean from dirty clothes because they were all jumbled together on the floor. Consequently, after talking for days "put your clothes away" to nobody was listening, I would be forced to throw everything in the dirty hamper and to the laundry room, both clean and dirty clothes. Guess how much the water bills were every month…. you guessed it.

We did not spare the rod and spoil the children when they were younger. We gave discipline the same way we received it from our parents. In other words, they endured spanking when they misbehaved. When they got older, they got taller than me. I became the "midget" in the family. I was five feet five inches tall. They were all "towering" over me, each over six feet as teens. Spanking no longer was my option for punishing bad behavior. Privileges were taken away as a form of punishment. Recently, the children joked and reminded us how we used to spank them for bad behavior. I always told them, "Yea…that is why you are successful today. Would you rather we left you to go astray?" Ha ha ha.

Making their beds up was another difficult task for them. After talking about it for weeks to nobody was listening, I mandated them. The beds must be made before they left for school otherwise whoever defied the mandate would lose play time when they came back from school. One day, one of the boys (remain unnamed) made his bed very nicely, then went under the bed to sleep. I went to his room for something which am not able to remember now. His bed looked like no one had laid on it. I looked everywhere but he was nowhere to be found. His siblings did not know where he was. First, I thought about those stories I heard about kids who snick out of the house defying their parents' wishes. Had my son left the house, but to where in the night?

Fear gripped me immediately. Where is he, what may happen to him? I assumed the worst. *"I know we ate dinner together but how come he is no longer in the house,"* I thought. Neither did he tell anyone where he was going.

One of his brothers saw toes at the foot end under his bed and called me. "He is sleeping under the bed!" He appeared comfortable sleeping under the bed! The noise we were making did not wake him up. He must have been doing this since I gave the mandate. I just did not know it.

Oh my God! What have I done to my children? Have I driven them into this insane behavior? Oh no, I have pushed them too hard! I said to all of them, "If you feel this way about making your bed, do not worry. If you just close your door so I do not see your room, I will be okay with it. And am not opening the door to look." I stopped looking in their rooms to check the cleanliness from then on.

My children were highly active growing up. They were close in age, everywhere for them was a playground and they liked to play tug of war and kick boxing. The saying "boys would be boys" was absolutely true for my boys. They played so hard inside the house, the same way they would outside until something breaks, or I started screaming to "STOP before someone gets hurt". We had big yards in front and back of the house. But sometimes their play would be spontaneous, and they start playing from inside the house.

A lot of times they knocked things down, punching holes on the walls, breaking dishes, cups, cabinets, chair, tables and so on. In the process, they incurred scrapes and bruises. They would hide the scrapes from me. I spent so much money on handyman services for patching walls. I was forced to learn how to patch the small ones myself, because they occurred very frequently. Except one, the mighty gape I had to get home improvement people to put back half a sheet of drywall they knocked out by the bathroom wall. Some days, I thought maybe if we had at least a girl, they would be a little gentler! Our kids love each other and us, and we love them too. There were times I thought they were not listening to us parents, not following instructions. I did not know they heard most of our admonitions as they were growing up.

Recently one of my younger friends expressed frustration about her children not listening to her. Another lady was lamenting during one of our women meetings, about her children not following directions and she did not want to spank them. My response was, not to relent efforts in giving them directions. Though it might seem they were not listening at the time, they would change as they get older. My children were examples of that. Proverb 22:6 said: "Train up a child in the way he should go, and when he is old, he will never depart from it". (KJV). King Solomon got it very right. We followed king Solomon's precepts in raising our children but not necessarily putting it in that context. At that time, I too was lamenting as the lady in the women's meeting, worrying that our children were not listening. All those worries were for naught. I could have saved my adrenaline and cortisone if I thought about it then. But it is well, all turned out well for us.

A lot of times I thank God for how well our children have become. When I visit my children's homes now that they are adults, and see how clean and organized they all kept their homes, I could not believe it. Those clothes that were always all over the floors in my home got properly tucked away in the hamper or hung in the closet. The clean and the dirty clothes are in their proper places. The beds got nicely made. Dishes always got cleaned and packed away. One of them once told me, "Mom let me do the dishes, you don't know how to do them," ha ha! I always tell anyone whose children are causing them exasperation, to cool down. The children are hearing you, believe me! I am telling you this out of my own experience.

Chapter 7

The College Years

Our three children went to college on scholarship having achieved good academics and athleticism. Robert and Paschal made the Maryland Terps Football Team under Coach Prigen. Weekends, we would drive up to Collage Park to watch their games. Our tickets were always free. We would first go for the tailgate and later watch the game. It was an exciting time for us, and we always looked forward to going to their home games. We very much enjoyed the tailgate with other parents of Terp players. The food, and the drinks were savored. That way we built up a network of parents of Terps players. We would do bus travels together for away games that were not too far, such as games played in neighboring states like Virginia and New Jersey. We had the opportunity to fly to different parts of the United States to watch their away championship and bowl games. We went to two of their bowl games, one in Atlanta and the other in Miami, Florida. We had fun and it was a wonderful time of our lives. The two boys were excellent students and athletes throughout their collage years and Robert finally became eligible to join the National Football League with the Ravens when he graduated.

In the spring of 2003, Victor was completing high school at Gilman school. It was time to search for college. He was a highly recruited student athlete. A lot of the great colleges in the United States wanted him. University of Maryland was number one, Stanford University in California, Ohio State University Ohio, University of Southern California (USC), Notre Dame Indiana to name a few.

MY AMERICAN ADVENTURE (2024)

Since Maryland already had two of our children, I believed they thought they had entitlement here. At first, I wanted Victor to join his brothers in Maryland. My rationale was more of a selfish reason, the distance to distant schools was too much for us. I thought about having to finance travel to those places to watch Victor's games. I considered the proximity of college park and the convenience of having to watch only one game for the three boys. Coach Pridgen convinced us to allow Victor to join his brothers. But Victor was not sure if he wanted to go to Maryland but was open to inquiry. He had done college visits to those schools named above except Maryland.

On the day of Victor's college visit to Maryland, one of the coaches tried to buy him over by giving him a gift (money to buy XBOX and video games worth $300). The gift was in violation of NCAA recruitment rules. No school should influence any potential recruit by any kind of gift. When the gift giving was discovered, my husband and I quickly returned the gift to Maryland. Maryland was banned from recruiting Victor from then on. As my children were local sports celebrities in Baltimore, that Maryland scandal hit the news media fast. I heard so much "garbage" and animosity people I did not even know were holding for me. Some people's comments were so caustic, such that one would believe they were jealous.... of someone they didn't even know.

On the radio, there were so much "thrash" people were heaping on my child and my family. Those commentators seemed to have forgotten that the genesis of the issue was an overzealous Maryland coach who wanted to take advantage of a sixteen-year-old boy with a stellar character. I listened to the radio one day, someone criticized the parents for not raising their child well! They did not even know me or my child, how could anyone pass judgement on me or my child?

For weeks, it was the topic of discussion on sports columns in the newspapers and radio sports. At some point, I stopped watching the news or listening to the radio until the news cycle was over. In the end, my son, Victor learned a big lesson so young in life...that there are always prying eyes on celebrities. He learned he should never be a part of such behavior again in his life. "Everything happens for a reason." University of Notre Dame Indiana recruited him after that

Maryland scandal, and he accepted. That was another great decision Victor made. Victor went to University of Notre Dame and played college football. Notre Dame gave him a good preparation to be successful in life.

College years were busy for us, my husband and myself. Going to games occupied our weekends. We would go to Maryland game on one weekend. Then we went to Notre Dame Indiana on the other. So, we missed some of Maryland games and some Notre Dame games. Our commute to Indiana was mostly by flying. A few times we drove. As with Maryland, we tailgated with other parents at Notre Dame. Some of them knew we came from long distance, and invited us to their tailgate without minding we were not able to bring anything for the tailgate. We were only able to carry hand luggage for the flight to South Bend.

We also made many friends with other parents of Notre Dame players. My son Victor was a scholar athlete at Notre Dame and earned himself some popularity in the school. When we missed his game, other parent friends took care of our son. On the weekends, we were not able to attend Notre Dame games, Mrs. Mattison packed every game newspaper article where Victor featured and sent to us. Mrs. Mattison was the wife of coach Mattison, Victor's defensive end coach. She was exceptionally helpful in keeping us updated regarding Victor's progress in the field. I am eternally grateful to her for that.

Robert graduated from college in 2005. He got recruited by the Baltimore Raven's Professional National Football League (NFL) to play in the practice squad during the 2005-2006 season. He played with the Ravens for three years. In the 2006-2007 NFL season, Robert was sent to Europe to play the NFL Europe. Injury to his left ankle cut his chances short to remain in NFL. So, Robert gave up his desire to continue playing in the NFL. He did not allow the disappointment in the NFL affect his progress in life. He had his college degree to fall back on. However, he did not believe Bachelor of Arts degree was enough to give him a high earning power. He went back to school to obtain his MBA while he was working.

When he was interviewed by the pundits who tried to get his perspective on his past NFL prospect: "My family took academics very seriously growing up - that's why we were at Mount St. Joe. I got degrees in Economics and criminal justice at UMD and had a solid foundation to fall back on" was his statement. Any parent would love to hear their child saying that! Paschal graduated in 2007 with BA Criminology and Criminal Justice. He is currently working for Mythic Inc and Oracle Corporation as Data Base Administrator. Victor completed college in three and half years and graduated with a degree in finance. First out of college, he was drafted into the professional National Football League (NFL) by the Philadelphia Eagles. Victor played for the Eagles for five years. His NFL career was cut short by injuries. He too had a solid foundation to fall back on. He went back to school to obtain his master's degree in finance. All our children are doing well in their respective careers and are very happy doing what they do.

 I would say my destiny has completely revealed itself so far. I remember the prayers I said on the 6th of January 1981, soon after we got married. I prayed for four children, two boys and two girls. God gave us four boys and took one back. I prayed for a good marriage. Ours was a good marriage, irrespective of normal marital ups and downs. I prayed for long life and prosperity. God has been faithful in keeping us healthy and prosperous. We thank Him!

Chapter 8

The empty nest

In the fall of 2003, August 10th, my youngest son Victor, went to college at the University of Notre Dame Indiana. My husband and I had dropped him off to BWI airport, to catch the plane to South Bend Indiana in the company of his friend Ambrose Wooden. As we were driving back home, I began to reflect on what just happened… was that my destiny? I thought about how God blessed my husband and I with three wonderful children and I thanked Him for the favor. It was a bittersweet moment. I felt freedom from raising children, however a cloud of sadness enveloped me.

For years, I prayed for this moment. How was it that I felt sadness when I should be rejoicing? I did not experience this feeling when the first two of our children left home for college. When we got home from dropping off Victor, the house was so quiet you could hear a pin drop. Those giant footsteps that sometimes felt like the house was shaking were no longer felt. I thought about what to do to keep busy and be distracted from that feeling except going to work but came empty at first.

The first month after Victor left home was the most difficult. The house was so quiet I could not stand it. I tuned the TV loud to obscure the house's soundlessness. It was at the time I had accepted a new job at the Veteran's Hospital in downtown Baltimore. My first day at the new hire orientation was August 11th, one day after Victor left home. I still felt sadness and distracted over my empty nest. I was sitting in a general orientation classroom with other newly hired employees. It was time for everyone to give a brief introduction of themselves. When it was my turn to introduce myself, in addition to discussing my experiences and work history, I shared my success story with the group.

I told the group how proud I was of myself and my husband for raising three wonderful, successful children. I told them our youngest was sent to college the day before, to one of the best colleges in America on full scholarship. I shared with the group my feeling of sadness when our youngest child left home. Most of the people there were much younger than me and have young children. I could see the expressions on their faces which appeared they were saying, "Is she for real? She should be happy not sad!" What I was suffering then was called EMPTY NEST SYNDROME. Believe me, I was happy my nest had emptied, but the feeling of sadness like I had suffered a loss was inexplicable to me. Hurray! Those years of stress that comes with balancing work, children's sports, homework, shuttling them from games and school activities, and preparing family meals were over!

I received an applause when I concluded my introduction. Some of the ladies said they could not wait to experience what I was feeling… meaning when they would be empty nesters like me. It was not long before I began to adjust and enjoy the empty nest status. With time, I got used to the quiet house and not hearing the gigantic footsteps. The best parts of being an empty nester were many. Not having to cook often like I used to do was my number one. Cooking for just myself and my husband required I scaled down the size of my cooking utensils to smaller pots. Our food expenses got considerably smaller.

Talk about cleaning the house. When the kids were at home, the house got cleaned almost every day because they tracked dirt and grimes on their tennis shoes into the house. No matter how much they were told to take the shoes off at the mudroom, they were not consistent with shoe removal. They sometimes snicked into the house with tennis shoes on when no adult was looking. Once they all left home, cleaning the house also scaled down to twice a month, kitchen and toilets more frequently of course. Laundry was scaled down to once a month. Hurray! consequently, house chores got considerably reduced. I had so much time on hand to do whatever I wanted to do after work.

Empty nest had its own shortfalls. Children's school functions and events took up a lot of my time when we were raising them. No more child related activities left my calendar scanty. I felt a lot like the children were my only life. I realized how much I loved being a mom. I could not think of what else I could occupy my life with at that time other than work. I again invoked the can-do never-say-never attitude. I asked myself, *"Have you spent the last twenty-one years of your life caring for your children, making sacrifices and neglecting yourself? You have been working so hard for many years to make sure everyone had what they needed and went where they needed to be? Why can you not shift the attention to yourself? Now that you have the opportunity to focus on yourself, you should take it."* It was time to pay attention to what made me happy and fulfilled not necessarily as a parent, but as a person.

First, I patted myself on the back for my husband and I for raising good children. My people say, "You take a horse to the stream to drink, but you cannot make the horse drink if he doesn't want to." Referring to our children, they made us proud by "drinking" up all the training we gave them at home plus those they learned in schools. They turned out to be mature, self-sufficient young men who were on their way to navigate the world with confidence. They all went to private schools from primary to high school. And all three of them gained full college scholarships. The monetary investment we made, the efforts and all the sacrifices we made on behalf of those kids were worth every penny of it. I felt like I have done my job as a parent, though a parent's job never ends as far as the children are concerned. When Victor left home for college, I realized how fast life was passing by. What should I do to make my empty nest a pleasant experience?

I began by taking stock of my life, an introspection, trying to get a long-range view of my life journey, and to evaluate my progress. Sort of review the balance sheet I drew years ago to evaluate whether my objectives were achieved, to know how much of it I accomplished and what I would like to do next. I thought to myself, life is too short so I should start with nurturing my health and wellbeing physically, mentally and spiritually. I was close in age to fifty. I thought I have earned the right to be called a woman in midlife…not in crisis but

MY AMERICAN ADVENTURE (2024)

in peace. I have led a remarkably busy life. I was always busy day in day out except the little time allotted to me for sleep. But my body was still in a clockwork mode. I felt I should always be doing something even when there was nothing to do. So many times, I accused myself, prosecuted and found myself guilty of time wasting if there was nothing to do. "There is so much to do Rita, you just have not looked". The feeling could be uncomfortable sometimes. Hello! Anybody else felt like that??

My first self-care plan was to allow myself FEEL FREE to do nothing when there was nothing to do! I stopped judging myself for time wasting. It took time to calm the adrenalin. I sat down and talked Rita down sometimes. *"There is nothing to do now. You have all the time to do the laundry, they are not many and there is only half a load today. You can do it next week when you have more clothes to wash."* I would check the fridge, do we need more food? Meanwhile, there were plenty of food that were still fresh. *"No, I ate that yesterday, I don't want to eat that again today."* I would cook more food. Food would fill the refrigerator and be thrown out because we could not eat all before they spoiled. I would become antsy, scouting for something to do. That was even more exhausting than actually doing the chore! All these feelings initially robbed me of the joy I should be feeling. I had to work hard on reminding myself that the children are no longer at home.

I develop a diet plan that I could stick with. I cooked less but healthy and nutritious food. I watched everything that crossed my mouth to ensure it had good health benefits. I exercised by taking walks with my husband. We enrolled in swimming at the YMCA in Randallstown. I would sometimes excuse myself to binge on TV watching, listening and updating myself on what was going on around the world and in American politics. CNN won the "contract". I read the bible more and my books on kindle. I also had a full-time job working at the Veteran's Affair Hospital Baltimore. With self-exhortation, I began to slow the adrenalin down. I began to cherish the quietude of the house, turned down the TV volume, postponed chores that were not urgent, connected more with friends and relatives, especially those in Nigeria. I began to enjoy my empty nest from then on. It was a wonderful feeling!

Chapter 9

Reaching the Crossroad

My husband and I sometimes reminisced about the years when we were raising the children, the high school and college years especially, how difficult we thought things were. We did not realize how good and fulfilling those years were until we no longer have a child in high school or college. Since the children all graduated from college, we have not done half as much travelling as we used to do. No more weekend games. No more excitement generated by all the hypes of game preparation, jumping in the airplane, and game day tailgates. Never a boring moment! But now we rarely travel! I cannot believe I miss those years. At the time, I thought we were drawn to so many directions. My people said, "It takes a village to raise a child." Other than teachers, coaches and other personnel my children have met along the way, we had no help in raising our children. We had no child-care help when the kids were younger. My husband and I single handedly raised our children. Sometimes I wonder, how did we do it?

I would like to send my gratitude to all the teachers that have been in my children's life from kindergarten 'till college and beyond. I will also thank the coaches whose influence navigated my children into the sports world. There were many of them whose names I may have forgotten. The most notable ones are the Cecil Kirk and Chick Webb coaches. They helped my children to develop the athleticism that helped them grow in the world of athletics. Mr. Roach in Holy Family School coached the children in the game of basketball. Mr.

MY AMERICAN ADVENTURE (2024)

Working of Mount St. Joseph High School introduced my family to the world of football. When I was ignorant about the game of football, Mr. Working schooled me. I have understood the football so well now I could referee a game! My husband and I joke sometimes that I could even kick a field goal at the 27-yard line, ha ha ha. Mr. Working told me, "I can get your children good in football, good enough to earn them college scholarship. You can become a rich woman." I claimed it in the name of Jesus. All his predictions came true! All our children had no school loans. They all earned their degrees with full college scholarship. How cool was that? I thank Mr. Working and all the Mount St. Joseph's teachers and coaches that helped to mold my children to the great men they are today. As for the rich part, I can only say we are extremely comfortable! Thank you, Mr., Working! Mr. Poggi of Gilman school, another coach that made a tremendous impact on my children, especially Victor. Mr. Poggi and all the Gilman coaches were great role models. The coaches coached the players in and out of the field. Mr. Poggi opened the world of finance wide for Victor. Victor spent all summer working with him in his investment company. Mr. Poggi also took the players on vacation to South Carolina for two different years. He made the players feel special. My family is so blessed to have known him. My family is so grateful to Mr. Poggi and all the Gilman coach for all the training they gave to Victor.

So, our children have grown up in America and our plan to send them to Nigeria every summer did not materialize. With the great successes they achieved in America, sending them there seemed it would distract their focus at the time. There was only two weeks break for them every summer and sometimes they liked to work. It took two days to travel going to Nigeria, and two days returning. It was not financially feasible to send them there every summer if all they had to spend was only ten days. After we struggled to squeeze in a visit when they were in primary school without success, we took a trip in 2002 April, before Victor went into college. We spent a month which the children appreciated. They were able to spend time with uncles, aunties, the numerous cousins, and learned the language but needed to sharpen them.

The children have become adults. They graduated with degrees in business world and doing well financially. None of them took the medical field or pharmacy we nudged them towards. We tried Robert and Paschal first. They both turned down being doctors.

"I do not like the long time doctors spend at work," was Robert's response.

Paschal said, "They take too long in school before graduation," was his dislike of medical field.

I then put all my hopes on Victor. Victor and I had numerous discussions regarding medical school. I told him how my birth family, the Chukwulebe family is a family of doctors and healthcare workers. I wanted to pass on the legacy to at least one of my children. I felt confident I got Victor to agree.

During Victor's last year in high school, I sent him to shadow Doctor Howard at the Union Memorial Hospital in Baltimore for six weeks. Dr. Howard is a well renowned cardiac surgeon. I thought spending time there could help him understand some aspects of the medical school. Victor said he enjoyed the time he spent there. He followed Dr. Howard and the medical students on rounds. He also went to the operating room to observe cardiac surgery. Anyone who knows my children will attest that they are big guys. All of them were over six feet as teenagers. Victor was even bigger than his older brothers. He had a lab coat with his name printed on the breast pocket (Dr. Victor Abiamiri). He was fifteen yet fit quite well with the rest of the medical students. Victor said people thought he was one of the medical students until they asked him a question, which of course he was not able to answer. When the six weeks was over, he came home and told me all he learned.

"So, what do you think about going to medical school?" Victor made "cut off the head" sign. I said, "Why honey?"

"Mom look at these hands," showing me both of his hands.

"What is wrong with your hands?" I asked.

"Mom they are too big. I was not able to pick up the instruments which Dr Howard was using in operating room. They were as tiny as needles. I am afraid I will kill somebody with these big hands if I become a doctor."

I said, "You do not have to be a surgeon. There are so many fields you could pursue." But he did not want to hear it. I was crushed! Not one of my children gave any consideration to medical school or even the health care field. My last hope has disappointed me. My legacy of the healthcare in my own family is now ending with me!!!

I gave up the idea of one of my children becoming a medical doctor or a healthcare worker, but I have hope one of my grandchildren will pick up the torch some day. My children chose the fields they love and are financially doing well. There is no reason to be regretful of my children ditching medical school. After all, there are five medical doctors in my birth family (The Chukwulebe Doctors) in Umuna Okigwe where I was born. Dr. Alexander Chukwulebe, my brother has four children and three of them are medical doctors, Dr. Alexander Chukwulebe Jr., Dr Chidimma Chukwulebe and Dr Ifeoma Chukwulebe. My other brother is Dr. Bernard Chukwulebe, a Doctor of Engineering. His son, Dr. Steven Chukwulebe is an emergency room Physician at the Northwestern University Hospital in Chicago Illinois. The other four Chukwulebe Doctors are practicing in Nigeria, something that makes me immensely proud!

Our children are now well established in America. Two of them are married with families – Robert and Victor. Robert is married to his college girlfriend Ihuoma and they both have two gorgeous boys. Victor is married to Andrea and they too have two gorgeous boys. Paschal is waiting for the right woman to come along. We have four grandchildren who we love and adore so much. Our children and grandchildren know Nigeria is their root and will always cherish it. They know their relatives in Nigeria and communicate with especially the younger ones in the media with plan to visit on their vacations. There are so many black people in this country who do not know their roots. Their ancestors were sold into slavery from Africa is all they know, but do not know what part. They spend money trying to figure out where their ancestors came from by doing DNA.

Our Children completed their education, earned their degrees and are working in corporate America. It is a good feeling!

Robert Abiamiri: Bachelor of Arts Economics, Bachelor of Arts in Criminology & Criminal Justice, University of Maryland, Master of Science in Technology Management, Foundation Technology University of Maryland University College. Currently working for Facebook as Site Manager & Leased Data Center Portfolio Manager, Regional Manager covering East Coast of United States.

Paschal Abiamiri: BA Criminology and Criminal Justice, University of Maryland. AA Information Technology & Database Administration and consultant at Information and Technology (ITT). Working for Mythic Inc and Oracle Corporation as Data Base Administrator

Victor Abiamiri: Bachelor of Business Administration, Notre Dame University. Master of Business Administration, Drexel University Philadelphia, currently working for Brown Advisory as the Principal Portfolio Manager, Brown Advisory, Baltimore, Maryland United States.

What about that plan to return to Nigeria? As of the writing of this book, the story of Nigeria has changed, but not for the better. In addition to the same old stories, the political climate is nothing to be desired. Boko Haram is killing people, and it is believed with support of the Nigerian leadership, funding their terrorist attacks. It is believed the Nigerian president, a Fulani man is behind them as he has done nothing to protect the masses. Fulani herdsmen are menacing the cities, moving from place to place in the Eastern region with their cows grazing on farmlands and destroying forestry and crops which are the economic survival of my people. Civil servants are not paid months after months. Hunger and diseases are ravaging the country. Kidnapping has intensified due to lack of jobs for the youth. Bad roads, lack of amenities remain constant problems. "It is not a good time to go back to Nigeria for good." When will it be a good time to return? It remains unknown! We have reached a crossroad and frozen at the intersection. Alas! My sojourn of the 80's has become a lifetime journey!

It is now 2021, forty years after I arrived, we are still in America. Not ready to go back next year or the year after. We have grown gray hairs. We are now senior citizens, social security and Medicare eligible. Arthritis is menacing our joints. Aches and pains are now our companions. Some of our body parts have been replaced. Our organs and parts of our body each has a different doctor catering for it. Each doctor prescribing pills to their heart's content. Our desert in the breakfast table is Cups full of pills. Our memory is not as sharp as it used to be.

Advertisements targeting seniors flood our mails, emails and other media: supplements, age defying products, senior living communities, elder care, wills and estate planning, home improvements, even burial sites to buy, are scary reminders every day that we have spent more than half of our lifetime on earth. The list is endless. We make frequent visits to the doctors, and always come back with more pills to swallow, with admonition to avoid this, that and the other. Now almost every edible thing is no longer good for us. Eat in moderation. Life in Nigeria was better when we left it. Is my destiny to spend the rest of my life in a foreign land where I have become a citizen?

We never thought Nigeria would disintegrate to the level it is now.... What can we do to save our Motherland Nigeria? Oh Motherland, I weep for you.

> Oh! motherland Nigeria, I hail you!
> The land of my birth and that of my ancestors
> With abundance of natural resources endowed on you by God
> Your flag features bold green, white and green stripes
> The two green stripes on each side representing your natural wealth
> And the white stripe in the center, representing peace
> Your coat of arms represents your national dignity
> And strength and fertile soil
> It features two white horses, One on each Side of a black shield
> And a red eagle standing on top of the shield
> The white Y in the center represents rivers Niger and Benue
> A land blessed with natural quietude,
> Free from earthquakes, tsunami, tornados,
> And Floods, hurricane, and volcanic eruptions

The pandemic of widespread corruption has ravaged you
Which every elected official vowed to eradicate
But instead, they dove deep into the very same malady
And boco haram activities have branded you
Synonymous with terrorism in the eyes of the world
Obscuring all the beautiful endowments you received from God.
You were used to be called the "Giant of Africa"
With rich heritage of multiple ethnic groups
The major three are the Igbos, the Hausas and the Yorubas
Each with its own native tongues and cultures
And her people with friendly and accommodating spirit
Doing all they do with gusto and exhilaration.
kind of exaltation that cannot fail to impress a guest
Your most intelligent, educated and hardworking children
Are scattered all over the world
Most doing well, and some not so well
With their can-do and never-say-never attitude
Building up the economy of other nations
Doing great things in the diaspora
While leaving you in decrepitude state
Coming home to the Motherland has become dangerous
Can we now call you the dwarfed Motherland, Nigeria?
The greedy politicians embezzle all the oil money
Leaving you financially desolate
And the mass public living in abject poverty
The rich get richer and the poor get poorer.
 Oh! motherland I weep for you, I love you!
I want so bad to help you, but I am stuck in the diaspora
But alas! I am only a twig in a mighty forest
For many years I got on my knees to pray for you
But it appears God has turned deaf ear to my prayers
Hear my cry oh God, for the deliverance of my motherland, Nigeria
Just as you did for the Israelites in the days of old.
Send forth a deliverer to save my motherland Nigeria
Like you sent Moses in the days of old

MY AMERICAN ADVENTURE (2024)

For I want so bad to come back to motherland Nigeria!
And all your children and grandchildren in the diaspora will return
To build you up like other developed nations
A nation we can all be proud of
When the industries and agriculture will boom again
Every man and women become gainfully employed
Children go back to school to learn.
Infrastructure repaired and working well
Roads and bridges reconstructed
Clean water and electricity in every town
Nigeria begins to enjoy the natural quietude it was used to
And regain its name as the "Giant of Africa"
May it happen in my lifetime. Amen,
Oh, Motherland Nigeria, May God bless you!
And all your children and grandchildren all over the world

Rita Abiamiri

Chapter 10

The Endemic of Racial Discrimination in America

There is racism against immigrants. Racism is prejudice which a person holds when the person believes that his or her own race is more superior than others. The person with racial prejudice most often believes the color of the skin is what determines superiority. They believe that darker skin colors are inferior physically, and intellectually. It is believed that white skin is more superior than dark skin. Among the black people, lighter skin people sometimes discriminate against darker skinned people. The racial discrimination I suffered when I first came to America was remarkable.

Racial prejudice was and still is endemic in the American society today. I came to America in legal status…as a spouse of a legal full-time student. I changed status when I decided to become a full-time student. Later I changed status again to resident alien, the green card, and five years later, swore the oath of citizenship in the days of President Clinton in 1995. I was never an illegal alien as they call it. I believe Black immigrants receive double doses of racial prejudice. I have spoken to many other black immigrants of the 1980's about my experiences of racial prejudice and injustice in America. Most of them concurred with me of having gotten the same treatment as I did. It hurts when the white brothers and sisters discriminate against Black immigrants, however it hurts the most when the black brothers and sisters of America….. those referred to as African Americans are the ones heaping insults too. One would think black Americans would receive other blacks with open arms but no. Is this America?

Not every Black immigrant is illegal. But a lot of times, all immigrants are painted with a wide illegal immigrant brush. I believe it is mostly because the mass public is ignorant about immigration system in general. Some people in America believe that the black people are coming to America from Africa because of poverty. Let me be clear to all those who have that belief. On the contrary, anyone who can afford to come to America through the NORMAL immigration system is not poor! It takes a lot of money to prepare to travel outside Nigeria; from preparing passport, seeking visa, qualifying for visa and buying the airplane ticket. So, when the Americans call legal immigrant names, they are misguided. Let it be known to everyone that people from the Eastern part of Nigeria (where I was born) who were able to come to America came mostly for education and not because of poverty.

Every legal immigrant from Nigeria was vetted, found worthy and qualified to come to America, based on immigration criteria which includes having substantial amount of money in the bank. For students, their families or sponsors must demonstrate solvency and sometimes pay one year school fees ahead of time before they got visa. Now tell me, why are the black immigrants from Africa, especially Nigeria classified with those illegal aliens who crossed into the United States from the southern boarder? Consider the poor people of America, those that live in the ghettos and on welfare, not many of them are able to travel to a different country to go to school if any. There may be people like those in Nigeria, but they never would ever venture coming to America because they would not qualify under any of the immigration criteria.

Then there is systemic racism also known as institutional racism. The debate about systemic racism in America has been perennial. This type is a form of racism that is commonly practiced within a society or an organization. Systemic or institutional racism was defined by Sr. William MacPherson in the UK's Lawrence report (1999) as "the collective failure of an organization or country to provide appropriate service to people because of their color, culture, or ethnic origin". In America, systemic racism is quite endemic. It could be overt or subtle. Most of black and brown people of America, be it African American or an immigrant from a different country, have suffered systemic racism in one form or another.

Systemic racism has historically been used in America to oppress and continues to be used to oppress Black people, Native Americans and other people including the Latinas, Asians and Mid Easterners. White people use the advantages the system offers them which is often called "white privilege" to maintain their supremacy over people of color... often called "white supremacy". I suffered various prejudices, all of which I do not have room in this book to enumerate.

In addition to the prejudice suffered at the hands of the "little people", at my workplaces, I also suffered what I would consider institutional racism, this time in the educational system. Years ago, not much attention was paid to pregnant women in schools regarding policies beneficial to them as much as it is done today. I thought I was treated harshly by one of my professors when I was in undergraduate school. I was always just getting over having a baby or about to have one every other semester of every school year. From 1981 to 1986, out of the five years, four children were born to us, one deceased as mentioned earlier. Almost all my children were born outside of the class sessions except Paschal. That was in the spring of 1984.

Most of my professors were able to make exception for me. Some allowed me to take the final exam after I had my baby. One professor graded me based on my class performance in midterms and class quizzes. Mr. Rhodes, a white man and the statistics professor made me repeat almost completed class because I was having my baby close to the final exam. I begged the professor to allow me to take the final exam before or after the birth of my baby as some other professors had done. He could not make an exception for me. His attitude to me could be interpreted as: "maybe you should have considered planning to have your baby in the summer holidays". Even when it was not articulated that way by the professor, I felt that was what he was saying.

But the following year, another student, a white woman had the exception made for her by that Professor Rhodes. He could have done the same for me. It was not impossible to do. He just chose not to offer me that assistance. I had to go to summer school that year to complete my courses, which was additional expense to a struggling student with family. Would I be wrong if I concluded that I have been discriminated against by that professor based on my race?

I also felt that there was discrimination by some of the professors in the grading of students' papers. It might have been there all the time but my first time noticing it was in graduate school. My papers always got a grade of B, time after time. I know paper grading is subjective but no matter how good my paper was written, it always earned a B. One day, I asked one of the white guys in the class to let me see his paper. This guy received a grade of A and when I read a part of his paper, I felt it was no better than mine. I have heard people say: "for a black man or woman in America, you have to perform twice better than a white man or woman to receive the same recognition". That statement is true because I experienced it.

On the job market, I have also been affected by systemic racism. I believe it may still be present in some of the organizations I worked. There were many times I went to job interview which I believed I was highly qualified for. White candidates with less experience and qualifications got the jobs over me. The things I heard after those panel interviews were, "Ghee your experience is remarkable. You are professionally qualified and did well in the interview. We have made our recommendation. It is up to the director/manager to make a selection". With positive comments like these, I would wait in anticipation for good outcome only to be disappointed.

Even when I knew I could grieve over their decisions, I opted not to, because I believed if any of the jobs was mine, there would be a Godly intervention that would make it favorable to me. I heard in the grapevine that before the job openings were posted, the prospective candidate would already have been decided. From the grapevine, I heard those interviews were staged to avoid equal employment opportunity litigation…I am not sure how true the assertion was, but I let them alone to their consciences.

At another time, I was working as the nursing supervisor for five years. I decided to change jobs in the same organization. Multiple openings came up and I applied for the ones I thought I was qualified for and experienced in. After having been interviewed for the five different jobs without success, I gave up trying. The sad part of it was the people who got the jobs were less qualified for the jobs than me. I would hear from some of the people in the interview panel that I have been passed over. People stopped me in hallways telling me how glaring that discrimination was. My response was not to worry. The job that was mine would come without me looking for it. In my private time, I prayed to my God which went this way: "My Lord, you have seen the prejudice I have gone through. You are the God of justice. I am no longer looking to change my current job but if you want me to change it, let that job come to me instead."

Three months went by, then I got a call from the chief nurse at the time. She said "Mrs. Abiamiri, there are two job openings in one of the medical units. I have interviewed you many times and based on your previous job applications, you are professionally qualified for both jobs and interviewed well".

I thought to myself, "Really? How come I never got any of those jobs before if what she said was true?" But I let her on.

"You will not need to interview for either one of them this time. I know also you are capable of doing both jobs. Are you still interested in changing jobs?" I said it depended on what the jobs were. The chief nurse said she had opening for the nurse manager for medical unit. She wanted me to take nurse manager position because she knew I could handle the affairs of that unit.

"What other position is open?" I asked.

"Case manager," she answered.

I thought about it for a minute, but she interrupted my thought.

"Nurse manager pays more money, I really want you to take it. But for the case manager position, you will remain in the same pay grade level. It is a lateral move."

I thought to myself, "Nurse manager position is more headache." The Chief nurse has been having serious trouble keeping managers on that unit. I recalled I had interviewed for that job three years before, but I was passed over. If she had given me that job three years earlier, she would not be looking for a candidate now.

Besides, I was three years older and did not have the same energy and zeal I had before to attack the nurse manager job. I knew that unit like the back of my hands. Almost all the employees there were always rebellious. I did not want that headache at my age. I did not care about the money. So, I told the chief nurse I would choose case manager. My rationale was because case manager was a lower intensity job. I was not impressed that she sought after me for those jobs. It appeared she looked for all the white folks around to offer the jobs and none of them wanted them. "Was this job offer a dump?" I asked myself. She is no longer prejudiced? I remembered my prayer to God, to bring my next job to me instead.

My conclusion was that God has saved that case management job for me and made it repulsive to anybody else. That may be why no other white folk took the job. Thanks be to my God, it must be an answered prayer. The chief nurse expressed disappointment for me giving up the nurse manager position. She offered me the case manager job which I did for the last eight years of my career before my retirement in December 2019.

Redlining is a discriminatory practice in which lenders deny loans, or insurance companies restrict services to certain neighborhoods due to racial makeup. It may include unfair and abusive loan terms, deception and other penalties targeted to the racial minorities. Is it then a surprise that black people are charged higher interest rate both in loans and credit cards? Looking back now, I too was affected by redlining in regard to our first new car loan. My husband and I were quite ignorant of the America system and so were quite vulnerable to exploitation. Opening of home care agency; a discrimination of its kind. Two immigrants opened a home care agency: MaryAnn Home Care. Discrimination killed it as enumerated below. With 1985 came the AIDs crisis. Not much was known about the disease. Fear gripped many people as death was everywhere, in homes and hospitals with no treatment in sight. I remember, nurses were afraid to care for a patient with AIDs. I also remember patients with full blown disease were left alone in isolation rooms with very minimal contact until they expired. If anyone cared enough to go into a patient's room, they dressed like the astronauts going into space… just to go into the room for about five minutes. Doctors examined the patient through the window and prescribed antibiotic and pain killers. The nurse would rush in and did what she could within a short period. Those patients died a miserable death with no friend or family close to them.

Some of the patients were never admitted into the hospital at all so they remained in their home still requiring care. Many home care agencies would not accept those patients in their system to render home care. A friend of mine, Dr. Adedayo Ekundayo, and I saw an opportunity to open home care agency targeted to the AIDs population in Baltimore City. We explored opening one, so we did the needs survey and found out it was a viable project. We heard some of the home care agencies in existence had opened many years back when most of the laws governing opening home care agencies were not strictly enforced. Those agencies had grown big over the years. We learned there were different laws governing staffing versus service agencies. Ours would have been targeted to service to the Aids population. I believe the government saw there might be a stampede in people taking advantage of the situation to open unregistered home care agencies. It appeared existing laws got more "teeth". Newer laws came into being.

We decided we would not cut corners and go all out for the home care agency. We wanted to follow all the state regulations and cover all grounds to avoid any future problems. At the time we were planning to open a service agency, one was required to write a proposal in order to be considered for the Certificate of Need (CON). Dr. Ekundayo is a PhD graduate from University of Maryland School of Nursing and so we embarked on the proposal writing. It appeared we did not understand the magnitude of what we were embarking on until we got deep into it!

We received the CON which would allow us to provide home care services. We opened our office in a small room in the basement of my friend, Dr. Ekundyo's house. We needed a physician coverage, physical therapist, nurses, nurse's aides, social worker, a pharmacy affiliate and a blanket insurance of one million dollars to cover us and all the employees we would hire. We were just starting off and so did not have any of those.

We were not able to hire staff at the time, due to not having enough financial resources. But because we were nurses, we began providing services, both skilled and unskilled, with hope to bill insurance companies or Medicare later which would help us financially. For us to bill, we had to have Joint Commissions and Accreditation Organization Survey (JCAHO) which is an accreditation body for hospitals, nursing homes and home care agencies. We had to have at least six months of services to prove we would be able to manage the home care agency and the patient load. At the same time, we both maintained our full-time jobs as we have not received any income from the agency, and also worked our regular jobs to keep the agency going. Needless to say, it was a very hectic time for both of us, as we both were struggling immigrants with families.

It was after the JCAHO survey was completed that we actually found out about the one-million-dollar blanket insurance had to be paid up front for the first year. MaryAnn was allowed to operate on a provisional basis until we presented all our affiliates: obtained all the contracts and showed proof of the blanket insurance coverage. We shopped most of the insurance companies we could find in the "yellow pages" in the United States. We could not get coverage for our "baby" home care agency. No insurance company was willing to give "Her" the benefit of the doubt. We went for a loan to pay one year premium which was ten thousand dollars; still that was not good enough…. two immigrants undertaking a venture this magnitude! How dare them????

MaryAnn was suspended from operation for not having insurance coverage and subsequently closed after two years. All the work my friend and I put into MaryAnn Home Care for those two years were never recovered. We lost EVERYTHING! What kind of discrimination is this??

In 1986, my husband and I decided to buy a new car. Previously, we had purchased used cars with cash. For the new car, we had to take a loan. The car was a Volvo 240DL and was brand new. I remember we gave a big down payment on the car plus the car we were using at the time. Yet, the monthly payment on the loan was still high, $300 per month and the term which at first we thought was five years, but then it turned out to be seven years. I think we were deceived at first, into thinking the term of the loan was for five years. That was because the payment coupons given to us initially would cover five years.

When the last payment on the five-year coupons was made, I thought the car was paid off. Lo! and behold, the payment coupons for another two years arrived in the mail. Oh my God! I thought the loan was paid off…but no. Our ignorance was exploited by the bank representatives. When I called the bank that financed the car to inquire about the extra two-year coupons, "Did you read the contract?" was the answer. We did not thoroughly read the contract on the day of purchase. Everyone knows the routine, the dealer representative presents the purchaser with a big pile of papers and then points to where the signature was to be inserted.

When I brought out the contract and reviewed it, I found out that the seven-year term was buried in the fine prints, and I was not able to see it initially. It took two more years to pay off the car loan. It was not made clear to us that the term of the loan was for seven years. We probably would not have accepted the loan term if additional two years were tagged onto it. The car dealership took advantage of our ignorance. We did not know if we had any recourse available to us to refuse the payments. So, we went ahead and made an additional two years of car payments. That taught me a big lesson, never sign any document that I have not thoroughly read and understood. On a lighter note, the car served us for twenty years before being given to kidney foundation. We were happy after all.

How do minorities perceive racism in America? The various experiences I have passed throughout my stay in America taught me what the mainstream black Americans have historically gone through in the hands of their white citizens. Racism has existed around the world for many years. In America, it has existed for hundreds of years. There has never been a day black people or other minorities did not get confronted by racism. America has laws that forbid racism and bigoted behaviors, yet people of color have often found it harder to get good education, good jobs or a nice, safe neighborhood to live in. Even today, a smaller percentage of people of color hold top-paying jobs in many fields and in the government than the overall population. Listen to the news reports and you will learn it has also been determined that more black people are unemployed or in jail compared to their white counterparts.

All these are testaments to the notion that systemic racism is what is suppressing the black people of America. I fully understand the plight of the black Americans and the restrictions imposed on them by masked and overt discriminations, because I have experienced it. As a foreigner in America, I took all the prejudice, discriminations and injustices meted against me as part of being an immigrant, I grinned and bore it then moved on. But for those born and raised in America, how do they perceive the racism, and bigotry meted to them? How will America make up for the socioeconomic inequity between minorities and the whites? How will America reconcile with her declaration of independence of 1776 (and later amended to mention women) which said: "We hold these truths to be self-evident that all men (and women) are created equal, that they are endowed by their Creator with certain unalienable Rights, that among these are Life, Liberty and pursuit of Happiness." If what those words as written in the declaration of independence were true, how is it that some people disregard the worth of other human beings on the basis of race, class, gender, religion and believe their own superiority over all others? These questions deserve answers.

Recent events caused by the political climate, have shone some light on the way the wealthy people continue to build their riches and prosperity on the "backs" of others who remain perpetually poor and beaten down. The rich got richer, and the poor got poorer. Take for example, the income tax cuts under Trump which favored big corporations and the wealthy. What happened to the middle class and the poor people? The tax cut simply widened the wealth gap leaving the masses behind. The pandemic of the 2020, also exposed the ugly truth about the huge socioeconomic disparity between the whites and the minorities. The disease (not worth mentioning its name here) killed more minorities and rendered many disabled with a lifetime health problems. Many minority businesses were destroyed and may never be revived. The killings of unarmed black men and women also put a sharp focus on the racial disparity as well. This book is not intended to dive into American socioeconomic politics and the mayhem that followed after the killings of unarmed black men and women, however I have to express my own concern about how all these will impact my own generation in America.

All three of my children were born in America. They are all American citizens. Like every mother or father of black and brown young men, I am always worried for my children's safety out there when they were younger and, even now that they are adults and no longer in my purview. I have to also worry about the safety of my grandchildren when they come of age. Right now, they have the shields their parents provide which will not be for too long. Will America be able to narrow the disparity gap by the time my grandchildren come of age? Will those who believe their own race is more superior than others come to the realization that all men are created equal and have the same unalienable rights, which includes life, liberty, and pursuit of happiness like them? I am looking forward to my children and my generations coming after them to not face such brutality at the hands of their fellow citizens, if something is done about it now.

To my American black and brown sisters and brothers, it is not too late to begin to make small changes to better your lives irrespective of the injustices meted to you. Small baby steps slowly get us where we want to be. A journey of many miles starts with one step forward. As said, most of us immigrants lived and still live through it. But no matter how much I got beaten down, I refused to remain beaten down. I was able to get back up on track. That is the difference: the resilience and perseverance with which I lived and still live my life in the pursuit of my goals. Develop your own "fight song" to motivate and push you along.

I have heard people express wonder about the kind of motivation some minorities have in life. The whisper was that everyone is put on this earth to make contribution to humanity. Are there some people created to just consume resources, to eat, take up oxygen and space on earth? What drives them to achieve any level of success? If people can come to this country with only one suitcase in hand and their brains, within a few years, able to achieve success, how come the indigenes are not able to take advantage of all the opportunities available to everyone? With free primary to high school education, discounted college tuition, and many different grants, how is it that there are some minorities who still do not take advantage of those? One can surmise that maybe the "brain" is to blame instead.

It should be made clear that free education and grants were only available to citizens of America and green card holders. Immigrants without green cards were not eligible for education funding. They were not eligible for health insurance in the community they lived. All the same, with perseverance, immigrants achieve whatever goals they set for themselves, no matter what adversity they go through. That was what I had to do the whole time I was a student until I got my green card. I worked and paid cash or check for everything from housing, food, transportation, child-care, school fees, and the like. The house and car were purchased by loans.

I also learned that the damage done to the psyche of some American minorities by racism and stereotypes is tremendous. Racism can have mental and physical impact on the people it is meted to. People who experience racism may begin to question their own worth. They may become depressed and worry about their own future. They may be driven into drug and alcohol abuse which contributes to their ultimate downfall. Some minorities are more likely to live in poorer, downtrodden neighborhoods and suffer from diseases such as diabetes, hypertension, obesity, strokes and other maladies. I felt bad that I was discriminated against when those insults were being hurled at me. But I never was depressed or question my own worth in a way that would derail my progress or take my eyes off the goal I created for myself.

Though I considered myself a victim of racial bias, I did not allow myself to be negatively affected by it. Instead, I talked to myself (soliloquized) to help me deal with the "trauma". "You crossed many oceans, rivers and deserts to come to America. I am a black woman, a Nigerian immigrant to America. If my being black OR a woman OR an immigrant is repulsive to anyone, it is their problem not mine. Rita, you are not going to let anyone cause you to abandon your quest for the good things America offers. You need to take the "bull shit" for now until you achieve your goal." Once I did my self-admonishment, this time self-admonishment worked, I said my prayers which spiritually and physically strengthened me and gave me more energy to move on. I also invoked the "I can-do never-say-never" attitude, my inherited "fight song" which boosted my morale, gave me more energy to attack the task again and do it even better.

It appears to me that some of the minorities who have seriously been negatively affected by racial discrimination have a completely beaten-down spirit. They were born in families living in abject perpetual poverty. Most of them live in homes with no good role models. Some of them have parents who may have been on drugs, or they may have been using drugs themselves or have been in gangs. The females among them may have engaged in risky behaviors, ravaged by venereal diseases, teenage pregnancy and child motherhood. The question is; how can "I can-do-never-say-never" attitude in life be instilled into people like those, to help them realize so much potential they have? How can one who has lived a life of failure be convinced into believing that all he needs to do is try a little harder to bring success to his or her life? How can one who has lived in poverty all his life be made to be receptive to any admonition about doing things to improve themselves? Would it be really worth the effort to invest the time in such people?

The best treatment for their low self-esteem and low motivation is to help them realize what they could achieve if they tried hard, and how much potential they were born with that is waiting to be unleashed. Start with working on the "brain". First, they need to start from their thinking about themselves. If they believed they were limited in life, then their life is going to stay limited. They also need to recognize that there is a higher power above them named God who created them and endowed them with innate talents which need to be developed. They may have suffered disappointments in previous efforts, setbacks or life may have tried to push them down, they should remember that God created each person uniquely with valuable talents. I have heard it said that "when one door closes, God opens another door. If all doors close, He opens the window". I am not sure where this quote came from but I applied it in my own life, and it worked.

There needs to be a change of that mentality regarding their reliance of the welfare system. Next, provide them the avenues to build successes that will help elevate their morale to achieve more. A lot of the minorities do not know the opportunities available to them, by the government and their communities. That may be where to start. With all the opportunities available to them in America, they should be able to find their niche in life and vigorously pursue it until they succeed. They need to learn how to do their own self-assessment to determine what they are good at and or what interests them and use it as a platform to develop life goal.

They need to surround themselves with positive people who are ambitious with achievable goals. It may be necessary for them to have a life coach or mentor to guide them. The challenge is being able to change their mentality. They have lived on welfare all their lives and have stayed comfortable with whatever the government gave them every month. That mentality is very pervasive among lower wage employees who are also on welfare. Their attitude is no consideration for tomorrow's needs "as long as I have food, clothing and roof over my head for today, let tomorrow worry about itself".

In my supervisory role at the hospital, there were times when I needed more staff to work a particular shift. Then I would make calls for staff and offer them overtime pay to cover staffing deficiency. "No thank you," would be their response. They did not want to work more hours to make more money, because they did not want their welfare checks reduced. Apparently, there were limits to the amount of money they would make which would result in reduced welfare check. That goes in line with the young girls purposefully getting pregnant so they can have more welfare money. Sometimes, I also wonder whether the welfare system is actually helping or perpetuating poverty among the people who are receiving it. What if the welfare payments stopped or reduced, would the receivers be motivated to seek other means of self-support?

I believe this issue has been discussed ad nauseum in many different forums and in the government but has not found the best policy to address the problem. This book is not a forum to discuss welfare issues. However, I was touched by the thirteen-year-old children having children. I am referring to those children who got pregnant so they can get more welfare money. I hereby give my humble suggestion on welfare that the welfare checks be made a bridge to self-reliance. There should be a time limit to stay on welfare. All able-bodied people on welfare should be willing to learn a trade or go to school and get a degree that can be used to find a good paying job. All education or vocational training should be funded by the government for anyone on welfare who wants to go to school or train in a trade. Even people with disabilities can be trained to any skill they can perform.

The issue of substance abuse should also be addressed. For anyone on welfare to receive welfare money, they should be willing to undergo treatment for substance abuse and be sober. There may be other appropriate policies that may address the issue and save the children from destroying their lives by having children early in life. I believe the Government needs to look for other alternatives to the welfare checks.

In my work experience, I have learned that some of the problems that our black and brown sisters in America have is loneliness, and lack of trust from one another. The lack of trust is the reason many of them are alienated from others. Some people have no friends or have bad friends that help them get in trouble. Good friends help each other in good times and in times of need. Young people, not having good role models can cost them their whole life. I suggest to young people to find a good role model if they have none at home. The wisdom that one can get from a good role model cannot be overemphasized. They should listen to the advice as they get it, not be rebellious and claim they know it all!

I am calling on all black and brown people of America to unite and be their "brother's keepers". Let us unite and fight the social ills against us together. I am also appealing to all Americans to STOP attacking immigrants, legal or not. All people in American should be reminded that EVERYONE in America (except the American Indians, the owners of American land) is an immigrant. Everyone's immigration status depends on when they arrived in America! Those who claim America belongs to them will always tell you their heritage was from another country....... Europe, Great Britain, Germany. Italy, Chek Republic, etc. Immigrants are contributing immensely to building the American economy, which in turn contributes to the strength of America. They are not taking the jobs the average

Americans want to do. The jobs that illegal immigrants most of the times take are those which no American indigen wants. Who will want to be picking cotton in those farms which the slaves did in the past, or be harvesting fruits and corn in the farms?

During the Trump administration, I heard in the news that there was a time when the southern boarders were closed, and illegal immigrants were not able to cross into America. Visas were held for migrant workers. Those migrant workers were sometimes the ones that worked in the farms. I also heard in the news that the farmers complained that the closed boarders caused them to lose multimillion dollars of crops that rotted away because there was no one to harvest them. The cost of produce escalated at the time, and everyone paid for it at the check-out counters of groceries stores. For the educated people, indigens or immigrants, there are plenty of work, so everyone is able to get jobs in the fields they are qualified.

Immigrants are not taking anyone's jobs! I like to see exactly how much money lost by American farmers on account of those boarder closures. That way the American people would see how much that action cost the American economy. Knowing that information could shed some light on how immigrants are helping to build American economy. Let it be known to all that the country needs immigrants. Suffice it to say that immigrants also create jobs in America. In 2007, one study found that immigrant-owned companies in America employed nearly six million people. Mary Meeker's report of 2017 predicted that the internet and technology trends emphasized the importance of immigrants in the tech world.

In that report, sixty percent of the most highly valued tech companies were cofounded by first and second-generation immigrants. They have also been influential in the innovation of some of technologies enjoyed by everyday Americans, take for example: Steve Jobs, a second-generation immigrant from Syria, and Sergey Brin cofounded the google. It was also reported that more than forty percent of businesses on the US fortune five hundred list were launched by immigrants or children of immigrants. We need to spread the love to all our black and brown brothers and sisters. We need to celebrate all immigrants!

Chapter 11

Eyes on the life goal is the key to success

Some people ask, how is it that some immigrants come to America with only a suitcase in hand and their brains, within a few years, achieve some level of success which some indigenes are not able to achieve? Using myself as an example, I came to America on January 17th, 1981. Between January 1981 and January 1986, I completed my bachelor's degree in nursing, and was attending graduate school, working on my master's degree. I delivered four boys, as noted earlier in this book, one deceased. I bought my first home after moving seven times in the five-year period due to child intolerant neighbors and landlords. I must say it was not by my might that I was able to acquire all that, I give all the glory to God for giving me the ability to achieve the much I have up to that point. I achieved much more over the years, but I like to discuss what I believe motivates an immigrant to work hard to achieve success.

I can only speak of Nigerians where I grew up...the Igbo land because I know them. In Igbo land, the value of education is considered particularly important. Every child is primed to believe that their success in life depends on education, so they take their education very seriously. Even some parents who did not go to school, know the value of good education. Parents would sell land property or anything of value if they did not have money for their children or relatives to go to school. Most of the time, the students start early to decide what career they would like to pursue, which helps them streamline their subject choices in the West African Examination Council (WAEC). With that in mind, the student would start early to plan their success in life. The first step in the plan would be to define their life goal.

A life goal is one's idea of his or her future, what a person dreams to be in the future. Successful people build their life around the goals they want to achieve. Anyone without a clear goal in life may not achieve much. That person's life may not have purpose and meaning either. Once the life goal has been determined, action plan to achieve it is implemented. Most of the immigrants from the Igbo land came to America mostly for education. Before coming to America, most of them have already completed high school and sometimes a higher education. They have already established a life goal they were pursuing which culminated in the completion of whatever course they pursued once they arrived in America. In other words, they were already on their way to success on arrival. They have already laid the groundwork for their success so all they needed to do was to design the action plan to complete it.

Again, using myself as an example, I already had a nursing degree from Nigeria. Even if I did not want to go back to school, I would still be alright. But I did, regardless of how difficult things were for me. Because I targeted another goal in life to get more education that would place me higher in the echelon of life. The virtue which I believe some of the immigrants have that helped them succeed was perseverance, the can-do never-say-never attitude. When things got tough, they invoked the perseverance virtue, as I was accustomed to doing early in my life. The student whose life goal is to become a pharmacist for instance will work hard until he takes the final exam to qualify as a pharmacist.

Being an immigrant student was beneficial in helping the student achieve success. You say, how can that be? The student was required to carry a minimum of twelve undergraduate credits, or nine graduate credits otherwise the student would be violating immigrant status and faced deportation. The student must remain in school no matter what obstacles they faced, as long as the school fees were paid, and the student had the resources to be in school. Besides, getting education was the main reason for the student to be in America to begin with. Why would the student abandon school and do what next? He or she was not allowed to work. An immigrant believed their success in school was existential.

Contrary to the Americans, other than self-imposed requirements, nothing provided incentives to push themselves harder. They could drop out of school at anytime there is an obstacle without any consequences to them. So, school dropout could be regarded as one of those things in America! School dropout in those days when I was in Nigeria was considered a stigma on the student and family. Unless the dropout was caused by parent's inability to pay school fees. Even if financial problem was the cause of dropout, the family would look for other professional handywork such as trading carpentry or plumbing etcetera to train their children in, so they would become successful people in their fields.

Think about what an immigrant student would face should he/she be deported because the student did not work hard enough to succeed in school. What shame deportation would bring to the student and the family who invested in the student's education, for the world to hear the student was deported because he failed exams or dropped out of school? Think also about those parents who sold their most valuable property in order to send their child to a foreign land to study. What if that child got deported because of a failure in school? The devastation the family will feel is enormous. Those were the motivations pushing the student harder to succeed.

I believe the endemic of school dropout common among black Americans could stem from the family dynamics. Consider the child born to the teenage mother. If the mother did not go to school, how would that mother be a role model to her children or push her children to go to the school and work hard in school? A lot of times, that child also has no father role model. Though the government has some programs to help such families, some of them still fall by the wayside. Regardless of how much help the government provided, the child having babies is more likely to face perpetual poverty, poor education, and remains on welfare forever which they pass from generation to generations of their family. Some teen mothers may not have the emotional ability to care for their children. The cost of teens having babies is financially devastating to the country's economy. There are numerous studies documenting this fact. (Impact of social and cultural factors on Teen pregnancy Akella, et al) is one of them.

Going back to the life goal, the child born to a teenage mother who never had any life goals other than having babies, would that child be able to plan for life goals for her/himself? The life goals I planned were what got me through the turbulent times of the early years of my life in America. When I decided to go to school in America, I laid out new goals and assigned a time frame to complete them. Going back to Nigeria after I receive my degrees was the goal that drove me to work hard and complete my education in record time. That helped me to focus and gauge the progress until success was achieved. Same as most immigrants. They all came to America with a goal in mind. A goal specifically targeted to a particular outcome…success. So, they all become successful and move on to get good paying jobs. Consequently, they begin to buy homes, cars, open up businesses, get married, have children and send their children to private schools, etcetera.

Their success gets viewed by some people in America as immigrants coming to America to take their jobs. But they failed to remember or understand some immigrants went through the proverbial "hell and fire" to get where they are. The jobs that the immigrants occupy are those they are qualified for. It is a fact that Americans with equal qualification and experience will be hired first before an immigrant. America is truly a land of opportunity, but the opportunity does not chase people around. He who works hard enjoys the fruit of his labor. The people who complain jobs are taken by immigrants sometimes are not qualified to do the job that some of the immigrants occupy.

Looking back now, I realize why I got viciously attacked by the staff of the nursing homes, they could be harboring the same sentiments against me and I did not know it. The staff of the Pennsylvania Avenue Nursing Home knew that I had the potential to succeed in America because I was already a nurse before coming to America. They knew I would eventually get my nursing license and start practicing as a registered nurse. Something they probably never would be able to achieve in their lifetime. Some of them had babies in their teen years and probably due to being bogged down by family responsibilities, might not be able to achieve their full potential in life. The staff of the Rehab Center had the same sentiment because I was a foreigner in their country "lording" it over them.

Having the eyes on the goal for success was "drummed" into our children too, the same way my parents drummed it into me. My father was a high school headmaster and earlier on in life instilled in us the value of education. When he died twelve years into their marriage, my mother became a young widow. Mother did not complete high school before marriage and so believed she was limited in what she could do to raise us when my dad died. Her frustration with limited educational opportunities made her incredibly determined to make sure all her children become highly educated. She continued to teach me and my four siblings that the death of our father would not be a reason for us not to get good education. I was the oldest of the five. My sister Maria came next. Then came the boys…Alexander, Bernard and Jude the youngest of us.

All five of us turned out to be highly educated people. Alex became a medical doctor. Bernard became a doctor of engineering. Myself, my sister Maria and Jude have master's degree. We all have done well in our fields and communities. My mother was an extraordinarily strong woman who taught us her children to be strong, ambitious and always reinforced our sense of self-worth and confidence in ourselves. She said you must work hard to become what you want to become. Nothing good comes easy! As Bongos Ikwue said in the lyrics of his "searching for true love" music. She never took no for an answer until the no is really no. I was in my second year in secondary school when my father died. As young as I was then, I watched my mother do all she did to provide for us and continued on the path my father had laid. I internalized my mother's "will-to-do" anything she put her mind to and to never doubt my abilities if I put a little more effort.

The goals were spelled out to our children when they were younger until they were old enough to set their own goals. I was involved in the school curriculum my children received in their primary and high schools. But when the children first went to college, I did not like the idea that the first two years of college was not targeted to the particular courses of study the student aspired to pursue. I preferred the courses be targeted to the course of study from day one, instead of making the student take subjects they never use in life. That is a total waste of the student's time. However, that is my opinion, I know my opinion does not count. Those were the reasons my people came from Nigeria and worked hard to succeed. As said earlier, they have gone halfway into achieving the goals they set for themselves. America was and still is a land where hard work pays great dividends. He who works hard reaps the benefit.

What about people from other parts of the world? You ask. What pushes them to work hard to achieve success? I believe those have the same motivators as my people. I do not know much about other cultures though. I heard that Asians help each other and their community to achieve success, especially in business. I heard that the proliferation of Asian small businesses in America is because Asian people are more trusting of each other and loan money to their own people to start businesses. I noticed this concept in hospital organizations I worked throughout my life in America. Most of the organizations I worked had people from many cultures working there. As said earlier, sometimes I branded them the United Nations.

It was a well-known fact among hospital staff that nurses of Asian descent helped each other more than they would do for people of other cultures. The "modus operandi" of patient care units was to assign patients to all the staff on duty. Once the assignment was done, the Filipinos, the Chinese, the Indians and other Asian groups would regroup to form other teams, who worked together on their assignments. They covered for each other at lunch time as "my brother's keeper". Working together helped them complete their work on time and so they always left on time. Some of the ones with good heart would ask to help those still working but majority of them did not.

Suffice it to say that life is like building a house. You must have a plan which includes the outline of how the house should be. The architect provides a blueprint of the house. The house must be built according to the specifications on the blueprint. Deviations from the original blueprint requires a redraw of the blueprint. How can anyone build a life without having life goals? Granted that a lot of minorities in general are suffering so much racism in America, there are still things they can do to live above poverty and not depend on welfare.

It has been said many times that America is the land of opportunity. That fact is well known all over the world. Anyone who works hard in America will be successful. Quite unlike some other places of the world where people work so hard and yet things do not go as well for them. In some parts of the world like in Nigeria, people find it hard to find good jobs after acquiring education to the nth degree. Some people will get jobs that paid anything just so they are working. Some do not get paid months after months by their government because the government money is embezzled by people on top. If anyone's life goal is to depend on welfare like their parents, grandparents and great grandparents did, they will remain in perpetual poverty and pass the poverty from generation to generation.

Just like the thirteen-year-old girls I met in the antenatal clinic bragging about how much more money they would receive in welfare payments if they had more children. That broke my heart! A thirteen-year-old mother has no motherhood skills. She may not be emotionally ready for motherhood. She has no job to sustain herself and her baby. She is still a child for goodness sake! The parents would probably be the ones raising the babies and the baby's mother. I would like to see how those children of those thirteen-year-old mothers have done in life. I wish them well.

Recently, I stumbled into an article in the Heritage foundation titled "How Welfare Harms Kids" by Patrick Fagan and Robert Rector (June 5, 1996). This article confirmed my speculation about the welfare system. I did not have any data to prove myself right about the welfare system, but my gut feeling told me the welfare system may be doing more harm than good to the recipients. Those authors asserted that it is welfare dependence not poverty that has the most negative effect on children. The authors further asserted that "a recent research by the Congressional Budget Office Director, June O'Neill showed that increasing the length of time a child and his family spend on welfare reduces the child's IQ by 20%. Overall welfare operates as a form of "social toxin". The more of this toxin received by a child's family, the less successful the child will be as adult". I was greatly troubled when I read that article because if that assertion was and is true today, why is America still distributing "social toxins" to her indigens? Would dishing out social toxins do not equate to distributing poisons to people?? Will it be accurate then to conclude that the social toxins would be another repressive tool used on the minorities?

One would then ask, why would anyone choose to be on welfare instead of working hard to live above poverty? Who would want their children's IQ to be reduced by 20%? Maybe someone like the thirteen-year-old mother who has been on welfare all her life and probably had parents on welfare too. She may not even think or care about the future of her baby at the time. One can accurately state the thirteen-year-old, and probably her parents or guardian are ignorant and do not know any better. I wonder if they are given a choice between a good paying job and remaining on welfare, what will their choice be?

Chapter 12

Learning from experience

I always learned from my mistakes and other people's mistakes. That means I try not to make the same mistake twice and also avoid any mistake I know other people have made. I can only hope that by reading my story in this book, other immigrants who are currently in America, and are going through the same trepidation I went through or those yet to come to America, will find inspiration and empowerment to continue chasing their dreams in America until they succeed, as I did. I want to share what I learned along the way, and the importance of always putting in one's best effort and focusing on what one does without letting anyone derail one's goals. If somehow, they trip along the way, they learn to pick themselves up, dust themselves off and continue from where they stopped.

Having negative thoughts will only bring the pain of disappointment. A small negative thought may metamorphosize into a huge "boulder" which will then be difficult to move. Very often, some people allow past experiences to keep them from chasing their goal. The naysayer in them would say, "what if I try and fail" or maybe "I am not cut out for that". The negative thoughts may stymie any progress they made or about to make. I want to inspire in the readers to believe that almost anything is possible if they work hard. If they would let go of past experiences, failures, disappointments and focus on the future, they stand a better chance of moving forward.

My experience taught me that a solid support system is essential for success in America. But a lot of times, that kind of support may not be available to an immigrant. In which case there is no need to curl up in fetal position and "throw in the towel". The immigrant should tap into his or her God given innate abilities and self-confidence to help plough through. Having confidence in oneself and one's abilities will help them overcome some of the obstacles on their way. Determination, commitment and a burning desire to see your dreams come through are the catalysts that are driving your effort to achieve your goals.

There may be times when it may seem you have impossible dreams. You say, "Hey, I have tried everything but still not making any progress. What should I do?" My suggestion is you give yourself some time, re-evaluate your goal to see if it is an achievable goal, pray about it, and get back to working your goal or a modified version. With your faith, (I assume you have faith) your success in achieving those dreams becomes a miracle. Bear in mind that the decision you make today, will affect your generations coming after you. You are sowing the seed for the future of your generation. If you sow a seed of mediocrity, that's what your children and grandchildren will inherit.

Working as a nurse was not easy. Initially making money to pay all our bills was my primary focus. My career span began in the days when America had the crisis of nursing shortage. Staffing agencies propped up all around and were offering a lot more money than hospitals and nursing homes. Working for the staffing agency offered no other benefits except the money. I joined two different agencies just to make sure I got shifts whenever I needed to work. The advantage of working for the agency was, there was no commitment to work until one signed up to work a particular shift. The nurse could call the agency whenever the nurse needed to work and would instantly get a shift. On the other hand, the agency could call the nurse to work. The nurse either accepted or declined. That set up worked very well with my family obligations and school requirements.

The other advantage of working for the agency then was instant pay. Once the nurse completed a shift and her time sheet got signed by the authorized entity in the institution verifying the nurse worked, the nurse could turn the time sheet in to the agency to get instant pay. It was very convenient. I always had enough money to pay our bills.

If we needed big item purchase, I would calculate how much it would cost and book a corresponding number of shifts to cover the purchase.

Working with an agency came with its own shortfalls. Since the nurse is not an employee of the institution, the staff of the hospital did not treat the agency nurses with respect. As an agency nurse in any hospital, the hospital got their money's worth out of that nurse. In other words, the nurse always got the worst assignments and worked harder than the staff of the hospital… called "dumping". I believe the reason the agency nurse always got "dumped" on was because the hospital staff felt jealous that the agency nurse was making more money than them. They failed to remember that the agency nurse did not get any other benefit. Their benefit was calculated into the pay they received. A lot of times they would not help if the nurse needed help. I worked for the agency for about five years. The nursing needs of hospitals dwindled in the mid 90's, getting shifts from the agency became increasingly difficult. That was when I took a staff position in a hospital, at the Johns Hopkins Hospital in Baltimore. From there, I moved on to different hospitals that I worked for throughout my working life in America.

Looking back at my life, I would say I did rather excellent. I survived the tribulations of an immigrant in America. I earned multiple academic degrees which helped me hold high positions in the healthcare industry making decent income. I was blessed with three wonderful children who, with our parentage have established themselves well in America. They all got multiple university degrees and are working in corporate America today. At the writing of this book, two of them are married and have two boys each making us grandparents of four adorable boys. They are wonderful husbands and fathers to their families. Our extended relatives are all doing well and some of them have achieved great successes worthy of bragging about. I cannot claim that all these successes are from my might or my husband's alone. They did not come about but for hard work, discipline and dedication from my husband and I, our children and relatives all achieved success as well with God's guidance. I give God all the glory for giving me the will to endure all the prejudices, the tribulations and still come on top. May His name be glorified!

Investment in the Motherland

In those turbulent years, while we were struggling to support ourselves, our children in America and our relatives in Nigeria, we deemed it necessary to invest in Nigeria. The idea was when we finally go back, there would be something there to fall back on. We considered real estate as a great investment, and we embarked on it. Then it was a great plan… I am yet to conclude if it is….

First, we purchase a three-bedroom bungalow in Owerri, Imo State in 1988. The plan was, once we get home, we would stay there and work to achieve greater things. But when going home finally in the late eighties was not possible, we began building an eight-bedroom mansion in the village in 1994. The house was completed in 1997. It was the first beautiful mansion of its kind in the whole village at the time! So, we had two homes, one in the village and the other in Owerri.

We were extremely happy and proud of our accomplishments…. we had secured our dwellings. The next step would be to invest in properties in the towns, buy lands and develop in the cities to build a real estate empire for us and our generations. It was a great way to build wealth. A lot of the Igbos we knew then had the same plan. It seemed like there was a competition to see who would build the most; that was what was in vogue then. My husband was always looking out for who built what and compared them with us.

When Nigeria moved its capital from Lagos to Abuja in the early 2000's, there was a stampede of land purchase and property developments in Abuja. We were tempted to invest in Abuja, but we were not "sold" on the Abuja investment because Nigerian political climate was unpredictable. I remembered what happened in the Nigerian civil war, when properties of the Igbos in the Northern Nigeria were destroyed, and some people lost their lives. We thought it best to invest close to home. We did not think Abuja investment was a good plan at the time. We decided to invest in the then Imo State, Aba was in Imo State then but currently has been assigned to Abia State.

We purchased an unfinished plot of land near Ariaria market in Aba. We were told the land had a high potential for future yield, if sold later or if developed. We believed it and paid for the land in full. The plot had a structure in it called "boys' quarter" which we were told was rented. A "trusted" family friend was managing it. He was supposed to help us complete and procure the purchase documents of the land. We were never able to get the paperwork for the land up 'till today. Neither did we or any member of our family in Nigeria claimed they receive money realized from the rentals. The agent who helped us buy the land initially passed away a few years later and so far, we have no document to search for the land if we decided to pursue it. As most Nigerians know, duping people in land purchases was and still is common. We did not know it at first that we might have been victims of land purchase fraud.

We had the documents for the bungalow we purchased in Aladimma Estate in Owerri. Years later, even when we had the papers for the land, one of my husband's family member was able to change the documents to his name by which he sold the property and kept the money. We ended up not having any property in town, not in Owerri nor in Aba, necessitating the need to build another house in Owerri…again? You ask. So my husband thought!

The new house in Owerri was completed in 2016, another beautiful home. Up to the time of the writing of this book, our family has spent time in the village house only once, in 2002. For the whole time we stayed there, we had to hire armed guards to keep us safe. At other times, I went to Nigeria alone, I could not spend the night in the house since we did not have armed guards. There has not been another opportunity to stay in that house neither has there been any opportunity to stay in the Owerri house. The house in the village is now occupied by relatives.

Some of our Nigerian friends had the foresight about the future of their investments and sent their children to go to school in Nigeria or made solid arrangement to have a trusted person oversee them. That way, their children grew up there, knew so much about Nigeria and knew where their parents' investments were. In our own case, our children have been to Nigeria only twice, each time we spent about a month. First time in 1988 when they were all under five and have no memory of that visit. The second time was in 2002 which they remember but have not gone back there since then. My husband and I have been alternating visits to Nigeria since the last family visit in 2002. But our children have not had the chance to go with us. Series of visits are now planned for us and our children to visit Nigeria in the near future. The village house needed a face lift. We have spent large sum of money to renovate it. I cannot wait to spend time in both houses.

Considering the political and economic climate in Nigeria, there has been more and more discussions recently about when it will be best to return to Nigeria. There are still kidnappings for ransom, corruption is everywhere, no good roads, no water and electricity, hospitals are not equipped, anarchy rules the day, and so on. We have raised our children in America. Our children know we have those homes there, which will be their inheritance when our time here on earth is up. We need to enjoy it now that we are still on earth. But we have been waiting for Nigeria to improve so we can move back, but it seems as though we have a long wait and no idea when the time will come. Very sad indeed!

What a big disappointment! Should we take the bull by the horn and leave United States? With concern about sub-par health care in Nigeria, I am hesitant to relocate to Nigeria even if it is what I would like to do. The children have interest in periodic visits to the motherland, but not relocating. At the time of writing this book, all that is reasonable for us is short visits. If all we use those houses for our short visits, is it worth spending all that money building those houses? How are we sure our children will be able to claim the houses in the far future? Could the houses be rented or sold in the future?

You ask. The house in the village should not be rented or sold because it is in the family land.

The house in Owerri was built with a section that has two-bedroom flats. Those flats are rented. The tenants pay once a year and a lot of times they fail to pay when rent is due because they have not been paid salaries month after month. The return on the investment is so meagre and negligible. So, did we make good investments in building the house in Owerri? This remained a good question. Did we invest those huge sums of money to build just "vacation" homes in Nigeria? Is going to Nigeria once every three to five years a good reason to invest massive amount of money in "vacation homes"?

Recently, there has been more discussions on the Igbo forums regarding the next generation of the Igbo children in diaspora. It is becoming clear day by day that Nigerian children born and raised in the diaspora will make their home in whatever country they grew up in. Granted the children know Nigeria as their root, it is very unlikely that they will ever pack up and move back to Nigeria. There is speculation that even those born and raised in Nigeria up to eleven to fourteen years of age, should they leave Nigeria, will also join those born in diaspora. This is very troubling. Nigeria is losing her human power at the rate with which they emigrate to other countries!

Nigerians are acquiring high level talents in many fields of life outside Nigeria. They are using those talents to build other nations leaving the home country desolate. Alas! So many Nigerians and their children in diaspora have become lost generations to the motherland! Even if things get better in Nigeria today, how many of the Nigerian immigrants will return and LIVE in Nigeria again? Is there a possibility that the next generation of Nigerians born and raised in the diaspora will relocate to Nigeria? Even those children who were born in the diaspora but went to school in Nigeria, when they go back to where they were, they never relocated.

To my fellow Nigerians who are having children in the diaspora, learn from my experience. There may be other people like us who did not raise their children in Nigeria, you will be in the same predicament as we are now. America, or any other place Nigerian children were born, will be those children's homes and Nigeria becomes "a place to visit", period! Even those raised in Nigeria, when they go abroad and stay for an extended period of time, Nigeria becomes a vacation place to visit too.

I heard a troubling story about a woman in one of the private hospitals in Lagos. I am not sure about how true the story was, but it sounded credible, so I am using it to highlight potential problems for parents who live in the diaspora with their children, or those whose children are in diaspora while they themselves live in Nigeria.

According to the story, the woman was a widow and had eight children. All her children went overseas: some were in Germany, some in Europe and some in America. The woman was alone taking care of herself until she became old and needed help to take care of herself. None of her children was willing to take her with them and care for her where they lived. The children hired live-in caretakers to care for her. The caretakers took the money and neglected her. The children came together to decide what they would do with their aged mother. They were all well to do in the diaspora, money was no problem for them. In the end, they decided to put their mother in a private hospital in Lagos so she would have twenty-four-hour care by the nursing staff. The woman had no sickness that required hospitalization. The children all agreed to contribute money for their mother's upkeep in the hospital for as long as it took for her to reach the end of her life.

The story went on to say that the woman lived in the hospital for a couple of years until her death. Once the children got the report of her death, all of them returned to Nigeria to bury her and left promptly thereafter. The woman spent the last days of her life not being with her children or grandchildren (like someone who was childless), most importantly on the last days of her life! The worst part for her was that she was removed from friends and other family members who could have offered some assistance to her and be with her while she was alive and certainly at the end of her life. She died alone in a hospital!

The children did not care about the wealth their father amassed through the years and left behind. None of them wanted to live in Nigeria and inherit the wealth because they were all doing well on their own. They left their parent's wealth to be taken by family and friends. So the lesson here is: if your children grew up in diaspora, it is important to have a plan for your final exit. If you are in the diaspora and building skyscrapers in Nigeria, be sure your children know where all those Nigerian investments are, whether they will have access to them and how they will be managed behind you. To put it mildly: "Onaghi ahia ahu ihe mmadu awuru ihe onye ozo" meaning, it is not hard before one's property becomes someone else's. Anything is possible in Naija! That was my experience, and it is something to think about!

Chapter 13

My Legacy

Going back to my mother's words earlier in my life, I completely believe mother was right about her concept of destiny. I would say my destiny has completely revealed itself. I remember the prayers I said on the 6th of January 1981, soon after we got married. I prayed for four children, two boys and two girls. God gave us four boys and took one back. I prayed for a good marriage. Ours was a good marriage, irrespective of normal marital ups and downs. I prayed for long life and prosperity. God has been faithful in keeping us healthy and prosperous at this time. Our surviving children have all established themselves. They are making the "American dream". We have been helping our communities in many different ways as we are able. All these are my joy in life, and I thank God for them!

When I think about my legacy, what comes to mind is, how do I want to be remembered when my physical life on earth is over? I wonder about what people would say about me, and what influence my life has had on the lives of other people. What lasting impact would I have made on the world for the common good? In Igbo land, the belief is one's legacy is one's children. How one raised one's children determined the quality of humanity one left for the world. No number of other achievements will compensate for not having children or raising one's children well. Inculcating into them the culture of one's heritage and good character were of paramount importance.

Your success in life without raising your children as decent human beings who will continue your legacy and contribute great things to society means you have failed in your duty as a parent. With that in mind, having come to America with only a suitcase in hand, and in two decades raised a generation of successful Abiamiri family in America is a tremendous achievement. Also, I assisted my brother, Dr. Chukwulebe and his family to emigrate to the United States and settle in Chicago Illinois. Regardless of all the prejudices, the trials and tribulations my husband and I went through, we held it together and brought our children up and instilled in them the legacy we want to leave to them now, and at the end of our lives. I believe I have created a lot of legacies in my lifetime and still poised to create more. For brevity's sake, I will mention only a few in this book.

First: The Fear of God. Our children were raised in the Catholic faith. They were raised to know God the father, the creator of all men/women and the universe, and His son Jesus Christ the redeemer of mankind, and the Holy Spirit, the helper. Our children were taught to accept Jesus as their Lord and Savior. Abiamiri and Chukwulebe families are families rooted in the Catholic faith. My parents were staunch Catholics who played active roles in their church communities during their lifetime. Abiamiri family is also well known in the Catholic church in Igbo land for their faith and service to God. The family has produced four men who gave their lives in the service of God as Catholic priests. Two Abiamiri Catholic priests live in the United States serving God in the parishes they were posted. One lives in Canada. The elder Abiamiri priest is retired and lives in Nigeria. The Children were thought to know Christ, read God's words which are in the bible and meditate on them to understand their purposes in life, always pray, practice their faith and join a Catholic faith community. As Joshua said in the bible, "As for me and my house, we will serve the Lord" (Joshua 24:15 KJV). That is our family's faith mantra.

Second, the spirit of giving: Our children were raised to know that the family loyalty is especially important, both core and extended family in America and in Nigeria. Our children have seen over the years how we were always helping those we left in Nigeria, ranging from children's school fees, car repairs, house repairs and so on. Those four am calls were not and still are normal occurrence in our family and they are always attended to. Part of our not being able to save enough money to fulfil our goal of returning to Nigeria for good is our extended family's needs. We had to help them, in addition to taking care of our own needs. Our children have also been gracious to contribute to helping extended families in Nigeria. They have always been told "family will always be there for you no matter what the circumstances are. Friends sometimes will remain friends in times of abundance and may disappear when you no longer have anything beneficial to them". We as a family unit have made it a duty to help those in need. We have contributed to lift some of our family members in Nigeria above poverty. Our children now have gift giving in their DNAs. My husband and myself are also the beneficiaries of their generosity.

Thirdly, Impact on Society: Our children were raised to make positive impact on other people. We were assisted in that effort by them playing college sports in the professional arena, the great coaches and teachers they had from primary school to college. Playing professional sports in addition to teachings they received helped them build lifelong friendships, good work ethics and empathy for people who need assistance or less fortunate. They have been contributing to common good in their communities. Granted leaving behind large sum of money to offsprings or to some people is everything about legacy, I believe having taught them good work ethics paid greater dividends as they are now prepared to forge ahead in the corporate world where they are able to make even larger sums of money which we would never have been able to provide, thereby propagating our legacy to future generations of Abiamiri and Chukwulebe families.

But, I am not happy that none of my children followed me to the healthcare field despite all my efforts in nudging them towards the medical education. I felt that I failed to pass that torch of caring for people in the field of medicine or nursing to my own children. On the other hand, I am proud my brother Alexander became a medical doctor. His son Alexander Jr, his second and third daughters Chidimma and Ifeoma are both doctors. His first daughter and his wife are nurses.

My brother Alexander's family is a family of health care workers. My other brother Bernard's son, Steven is a medical doctor. There are five doctors in the Chukwulebe family and more may be coming up in the future. So, my birth family compensated for what I missed by my children ditching the health care field. It is heartening to know they are in the fields they love and that is all that matters.

My husband and I are proud patriarch and matriarch of our family in America. We have succeeded in building up Abiamiri and Chukwulebe families in the United States of America. We gave it our "all". We sowed the seeds for our children, grandchildren and great grandchildren to do great things in life. We laid good foundation and passed hard work ethics, determination and persistence to our children. We will be leaving our family's outlook better than we had it. Our children, grandchildren and great grandchildren will never go through what we went through to make it in life. Regardless of how all the aches and pains I feel now from all the work I did in life; I am grateful to God for keeping me healthy to enjoy a decent retirement. We represented our ancestors well in having children and raising them to be people who will contribute great things to humanity and that is …our legacy, MY DESTINY.

My professional legacy: I am a professional nurse and I love being a nurse. What will my professional legacy be when my life is viewed in the rear-view mirror? Reflecting on the profession I spent most of my life in; the Nursing profession, in other words, what impact have I made on nursing profession which people will remember me by? To answer this question, it is almost like writing my resume. Recently I tried to update my resume. I found out that it was close to twelve pages long. I had to omit so much information in order to make it concise and easy to read. As everyone knows, long resume gets boring to anyone reading it

The legacy of caring: I am glad I have made and still prepared to make a lot more impact on people in my forty-five years of caring for and educating the next generation of nurses. My career has primarily focused on caring for the sick and the needy, education for the nurses of tomorrow and advocacy for those whose voices are inaudible for one reason or another. My professional journey has afforded me the ability to make my mark on this world primarily because of those who supported me in my quest to becoming a nurse, those who taught me in nursing schools, graduate schools and clinical settings, and those who advocated for me to developing talents that afforded me the opportunity to change other people's lives for the better. I thank them for everything they did to help me become a nurse and to practice nursing.

There is no better joy for a nurse than receiving appreciation in words or notes from patients or family members of a patient who was snatched back to life from the jaws of a devastating illness. When I worked in the intensive care unit at the Bon Secours Hospital Baltimore, there were moments when it seemed futile to continue care for such patients. It seemed to me then that those patients were literally snatched back to life from the strong arm of diseases! At that moment, the nurse in addition to being a nurse also became the mother, the comforter or whomever she/he needed to be in order to relieve the pain and agony of their patients' illnesses. When they came back to life, they never forgot the caring they received. I felt fulfilment in my job and the legacy I was creating in those days.

In most leadership roles I assumed throughout my nursing career, I worked hard to make sure our patients received excellent care and kept communication channels open, so all staff had access to me. I encouraged so many people to pursue higher education in nursing in order to enjoy life fulfilment and increase their earning power. I mentored so many staff both those in different levels of their education and the clinical staff on my units. It gave me so much joy when I got notes of appreciation for the help I rendered or the encouragement I provided which pushed them to seek higher education. I also enjoyed the time I was a member of faculty at Coppin University. That time gave me a great opportunity to provide education for nurses in addition to the education I provided on the clinical arena.

I also belong to multiple professional associations such as: American Nurses Association, American case management association, Alumni of Association of Critical Care Nursing, University of Baltimore Alumni, Towson University Alumni, Nigerian Nurses and midwifery Association. I have membership in various faith-based organizations: Sacred Heart Catholic Parish Glyndon Maryland, Holy family Catholic church Parish in Randallstown Maryland, Nigerian Igbo Catholic Community in diaspora, Baltimore Chapter, Nigerian Igbo Catholic Community Christian Women Organization (NICCCWO), and Onuimo in Diaspora.

It is my wish to give back to society both in America and in Nigeria. My people in Nigeria are in need of so much help. I have started making small efforts to fulfil that desire. I have participated in medical missions with the help of other people in my community organized to help my people in Nigeria. We contributed to their financing and successful execution. Myself and some people in my kindred living in diaspora have plans for more medical missions and other help. I make donations to all my school alumni annually, to other charity organizations such as the kidney foundation, cystic fibrosis foundation, asthma and allergy association, Arch Diocese of Baltimore fund raising appeals, St Jude's Children's Hospital, and Catholic charities. I pray to God to give me long life, strength, the resources I can use to continue to support the charity organizations as I have done over the years and help make the world a better place, so help me God…Amen.

Chapter 14

My life regrets

I consider my life in America a great success. Regardless of all the difficulties, tragedy and prejudices I endured, I did not let them derail my progress. However, I cannot say I got everything I wanted out of my adventure. First in my mind is not being able to return to Nigeria for good before now. After over four decades in the diaspora, it seems that l will remain in the diaspora much longer than I wanted. All the problems in Nigeria have made it difficult for most people in the diaspora to pack up and go. Whether I will be able to go back in the future is yet to be determined.

Secondly, I put too much physical and emotional pressure on myself by working too hard to make the American dollar. Putting so much "milage" on my body (wear and tear) to all my joints, was caused by constant pushing and pulling heavy hospital beds and stretchers with patients in them, during the early and middle parts of my nursing career. Working in intensive care unit for over ten years was rewarding but took its toll. The high stress of working in a highly dynamic environment with all its unpredictability was not good for the "nerves".

Maybe one would consider me a workaholic then, especially during the time our children were in school. Our children all went to private schools from primary to high school. Being able to pay the school fees and have money left for other needs meant I had to make the money. Now, I am older and paying the price by arthritis ravaging many of my major joints. Left knee has been replaced and the orthopedic doctor certified the right knee and left shoulder as needing replacement too. I have had cataracts removed from both eyes and replaced with artificial lens earning me 20-20 vision, a great improvement from my previous blurry view of the world.

I put brakes on any more replacements for now. If everything I was told needed replacement were replaced, I would become a bionic woman, ha ha. Though I am generally healthy and strong, I still experience some Tylenol moments. I am putting all these out there, so others should learn from my experience. Yes, the health care industry offers good pay and flexibility most families need. It is particularly important for one to take care of one's joints and body if one has to push hospital beds and stretchers with patients in them. It is not much different than a professional football player who played in a league for ten years or more. The body takes its toll! When one is young, one does not feel the toll as much. However as one hits fifty, the joints begin to ache, and then "hell" breaks loose.

Thirdly, we did not teach our children the Igbo language when they were younger. They are learning it now that they are older which is a little more difficult for them. I have an explanation for why my husband and I initially decided to speak only English to them when they were younger… not to say it was a good explanation. Our oldest son had delayed speech. He was three years old and not verbal. His hearing and comprehension were tested and found intact, but he was not verbalizing words… not even yapping like children do.

After medical checkups, he was declared healthy, and the doctor said he would speak at his own time. We were anxious to have him speak, not speaking at three years old especially when we saw other children of his age and younger ones rattling words made us think; would he be dumb? We were not waiting for his own time. So, we made up our own diagnosis, "Maybe he got confused as to which language to speak since we were mixing Igbo and English languages in the household." We figured it out that it was best to speak only English in the house as we thought English was the language he needed to get around in America.

Even when the doctor told me at many other doctor visits that he would catch up with his speech when he was ready, I was skeptical.

That was a big mistake! Once he started Pre-K, he started talking after third day in school. He was articulating words well to my utter amazement. It appeared he knew the words already. But why was he not speaking? I thought he saw other kids speaking and realized speaking was not what only moms and dads did!

In our ignorance, we failed to go back to multi language family we were. As we all Igbo indigenes know, Igbo language is a little difficult because one word can mean different things: For example, using the word "akwa" when translated into English can mean bed, crying, clothes, or egg. The intonation used to pronounce akwa is what determines the context in which the word is used. Another example is egbe which can mean gun, eagle, or kite. Another example is Igwe, meaning iron, heaven or the village chief. With these difficulties, I am proud of my children's efforts in learning the language now that they are older. They are working hard to perfect it, and also helping their own children to learn it too. I urge people to learn from my experience. Continue to speak our mother tongue to your children and let them speak it too. I hear some parents say, "Oh they understand but cannot speak Igbo." Understanding and not speaking is not good enough. If your child has delayed speech as mine did, be patient with him or her as long as the doctor says the child is healthy. The child will speak "at his/her own time".

The Next Chapter of my life

As the years go by, the meaning of retirement continues to change. For some people, retirement could mean the end of full-time work and a complete transition to leisure activities. For others, it is an opportunity to create an ideal future. They may want to include work, volunteering, starting a business or travelling. Retirement readiness is like planning life all over again. It can depend on both financial and non-financial considerations. Just like setting life goals, the retiree needs to revisit his or her values, vision and goals, re-evaluate financial strength and ability to afford the retirement plans chosen. As for being able to afford the next phase of life, one would have saved enough money to last the remaining part of one's life. Talk to any financial specialist, one would hear he or she needs to save up to twenty times one's salary during his or her working years. I wonder how many people can do that!

The other financial support in retirement is if one lived long and reached the age of sixty-five when one qualifies for social security income, assuming the person contributed to social security in America. It is a well-known fact that social security covers less than seventy-five percent of the individual's salary. The person has to find a way to make up twenty-five percent in retirement to maintain the lifestyle he or she has lived. The United States Veteran's Hospital where I spent the last eighteen years of my career was very good at preparing employees for retirement. They provided series of retirement education and encouraged employees to attend starting five years before retirement. The program was very helpful to me. I learned so much information that helped me make very good financial decisions which are beneficial today. I am grateful to God that I retired relatively young and in good health regardless of all the aches and pains of daily living. I believe I still have a lot of life in me to live, offer the world and I plan to take advantage and live it fully. I believe I am well prepared for the next phase of my life, both financially and non-financial. My social security and veteran's administration retirement pension are sufficient to carry me through, giving me time to pursue other interests without going to work again.

My retirement plans are: first of all to be there for my family, assist my children in raising my grandchildren, volunteering in the church and my community, travel all over the world where travelling is safe, and help my people in Nigeria by participating in medical missions and fund raising for big palliative projects. I am very passionate about educating the next generation of nurses. I plan to go back to teaching in the nursing school in Nigeria. However, I will not be able to achieve that until the problems of insecurity and other societal problems in Nigeria are solved. I am patiently waiting for that time……

To my parents: Mr. Albert and Mrs. Florence Chukwulebe, I thank you for giving birth to me and my siblings, Maria, Alexander, Bernard and Jude, and loving us with unconditional love. Father, God took you to eternity before you could see what we, your children have become and how we are propagating your legacy to the generations that follow. I thank you for believing in me and inspiring me to do greater things. Father, you left us so early in life. Even with foggy memory of you, I remember you were an extraordinarily strong influence in your children's lives. The seeds of faith in God, hard work, perseverance and determination which you planted into us formed the foundation with which we live our lives today. The fortitude, strength and excellent spirit are all virtues which we are passing down to the next generation.

Mother you were beautiful inside and out. You had such tender heart filled with kindness and compassion for humanity. Your faith in God was as solid as a rock. Mother was a prayer warrior. She organized a prayer group who came together in our house to pray on Mondays, Wednesdays, and Fridays. She organized the young women of the Legion of Mary and taught them life lessons, ranging from humility, good character, hard work and marriage preparation. Mother was likened to Prophetess Anna in the bible, a widow who spent days and nights worshiping God in the temple. Mother you taught us your children how to pray. I always watched you pray every day for us and for others. Mom openly expressed her faith and devotion to God which earned her the most pious woman in Okigwe diocese in 1993.

Mama as we called her was a courageous woman of God. She helped so many men and women to convert to Christianity from idolators. Mama organized a crusade that went around Umuna town with the then Catholic Priest - asking all the idolators to give up their idols. The idols were collected in one location and burned. Many of those idolators got baptized and the couples among them who were not married in the church, all received the sacrament of matrimony. She was said to be a "terror" to idolatry. Mama was instrumental in helping to install Umuna Okigwe as a parish by the then Bishop of Okigwe diocese Rev Dr. Anthony Ilonu.

MY AMERICAN ADVENTURE (2024)

I remember well that mother started her ministry in the early 70's right after the Nigerian civil war. I have heard you mom preaching to your fellow women and others about the one true God, even when your own life appeared to be in shambles due to the death of your husband. Mama provided counselling to anyone that needed it especially those young married women. Mother did a lot of remarkable things in our community. For example, she saved one of our cousins from being killed at birth by the barbaric practices of our people which were very rampant then. The story may sound like a folklore, but it was true. When this kid's mother was in labor, my mother and other women were taking her to the Umuna maternity home. The maternity was about five miles away and there was no vehicle they could hire to take the pregnant woman to the maternity, so they decided to walk.

On their way, the woman could not walk any further once they reached the village deity, okwara oha ukwu. She delivered the baby feet first (breach delivery) in front of the deity. The woman's father in-law declared it an abomination and said the child should not be brought home to his family because he came by feet and not by head, the normal way of birth. "He who comes to his home head first is considered his, and he who comes to his home by feet is considered a stranger". The woman that gave birth abandoned the child in front of the deity, went back to her father's house and refused to return to her husband and child. My mother brought the child home and helped his paternal grandmother take care of him until he became a toddler. He is alive and healthy at the time of writing this book. His mother never came back to her husband and it was reported to us that she had remarried.

I would not be who I am today without the seeds my mother and father sowed in my life. I will continue with the help of God to spread the seeds of love, kindness, faith in God, and compassion to our generations and to humanity at large, as you did in your lifetime. So help me God!

About the Author

Rita C Abiamiri (Nee Chukwulebe) was born and raised in Igbo land, in the Eastern part of Nigeria, in a village called Umuezeala Umuna Okigwe in the Onuimo local government area. She began her nursing career in Nigeria after graduating from Mater Misericordiae School of Nursing Afikpo, then in Imo State Nigeria in 1977. Afikpo is currently in Ebony State, Nigeria. She also graduated from the School of Midwifery in 1979 at the same school. She worked as a midwifery educator at the Holy Rosary Hospital Emekuku after graduation for about a year before leaving that job to get married. Soon after her marriage, she emigrated into United States in 1981 when she joined her husband Dr. Peter Abiamiri who, at the time was studying to obtain his doctoral degree. While in the United States, Rita earned her bachelor's in nursing administration from University of Baltimore in 1984, and master's degree in nursing administration from Towson State University in Towson Maryland in the year 1987.

Rita worked in various hospitals within the Baltimore Metropolitan area throughout her career in the United States, holding various positions, from lower-level staff to management. She was also an adjunct professor at Coppin State College for many years. Her career spanned a total of thirty-eight years in the US and forty-two years altogether. She retired in December 2019, after spending the last eighteen years of her nursing career working for the United States Veteran's Administration Hospital in Baltimore, Maryland where she held various leadership positions as well. She received multiple awards of excellence in nursing from multiple hospitals. She is a member of American Nurses' Association, member emeritus of American critical care nursing and various social organizations within her community.

Rita enjoys travelling, reading books, and enjoying music in her spare time. She and her husband have three adult male children and four grandchildren at the time of this book writing. She lives in Baltimore, Maryland with her husband.

Special acknowledgement and gratitude

All the Teachers and Couches who taught and coached my children throughout their adolescent and young adult years. Their good mentorship helped to develop my children into the successful men they are today.

All the Teachers of St Mary's School Govan in Baltimore
All the Teachers of Holy Family School in Randallstown
All the teachers in Mount St Joseph high school Baltimore
All the teachers in Gilman high school Baltimore
Cecil Kirk, coach: Mr. Melvin.
Chick Webb Coach: Mr. Coach O'Neil
Holy Family Coach: Mr. Roach
Mount St Joseph's High School Basketball Coach: Mr. Clatchey
Mount St Joseph High School Football Coach: Mr. Mike Working
Gilman High School Coach: Mr. Biff Poggi
All the Teachers and Coachers of University of Maryland College Park
All the Teachers and Coaches of Notre Dame University Indiana
All the others whose names I have forgotten.
May God bless Bless you all!

About the Book

This book is one of its kind, written by an immigrant who experienced firsthand the real-life struggles of an immigrant in America. It exposed the truth about the real struggles some immigrants endure when they initially set foot in American soil. The reader will be intimated on how difficult things could be for some immigrants, especially those who go to America with pre-conceived idea that America is the land free of struggles. Those who plan to go to America thinking that money is easy to come by may be royally disappointed after spending a short time in America. The author wrote from personal experiences of the difficulties she encountered, some of which could have derailed her goals and aspirations. In spite of all odds, her courage, perseverance, and tenacity helped her overcome and become successful in achieving the American dream.

On the pages of this book, the author passionately described examples of various adversities she endured which included racism, and discrimination. Racism and discrimination were and still are endemic in American society. The author emphasized the importance of hard work, believing in oneself, having faith in God and persistence, as the factors that helped her navigate her challenges successfully. This book is a good resource for anyone who has plans to emigrate or go to America for any reason, or to stay for an extended period of time. Going through prejudice or discrimination is like a "rite of passage" which most immigrants must go through before making the American dream. The reader will be well prepared to be pleasantly surprised if he or she fails to experience any of those or similar challenges as the author described…

This book is dedicated to Henry Abiaziem Abiamiri, our first son. His life was cut short by a ghastly accident in October 1982. He was one year old.

www.ingramcontent.com/pod-product-compliance
Lightning Source LLC
LaVergne TN
LVHW012022060526
838201LV00061B/4408